From the Beaches to the Baltic

From the Beaches to the Baltic

The Story of "G" Company 8th Battalion the Rifle Brigade during the campaign in North-West Europe

The Naval & Military Press Ltd

Published by

The Naval & Military Press Ltd
Unit 5 Riverside, Brambleside
Bellbrook Industrial Estate
Uckfield, East Sussex
TN22 1QQ England

Tel: +44 (0)1825 749494

www.naval-military-press.com
www.nmarchive.com

In reprinting in facsimile from the original, any imperfections are inevitably reproduced and the quality may fall short of modern type and cartographic standards.

THIS BOOK IS DEDICATED TO THE MEMORY
OF
THE FORTY-ONE MEMBERS OF THE COMPANY
WHO MADE THE SUPREME SACRIFICE

"When you go home tell them of us and say
For your tomorrow we gave our today."

Foreword

It is with great pleasure that I write this short foreword to the story of "G" Company, 8th Battalion The Rifle Brigade, during the campaign in North-West Europe.

There may be some readers of this book who do not fully understand the implications of being part of a Motor Battalion such as 8th Rifle Brigade. Every member of a Motor Battalion must be an expert in every conceivable infantry role. A tall order. That a variety of roles are given to them is well brought out in this book, but I should like to add that they were all done well and with a magnificent spirit.

The morale of this unit was very severely tested; prolonged action and many disappointments. But whatever the task given, no matter how unexpected nor how distasteful, it was carried out with enthusiasm and determination, and it was this spirit which did so much to defeat the enemy. I visited 8th Rifle Brigade many times, both at rest and during operations. It was a pleasure and a pride always to find, no matter what the circumstances, such an obvious determination to overcome all difficulties and not to miss any opportunity of dealing a blow to the enemy.

In conclusion, let me say that this unit did a very great deal towards the successes achieved by 11th Armoured Division as a whole, and that I was both proud and thankful to have them under my command.

Major-General,
Commander,
11th Armoured Division.

GERMANY,
December, 1945.

Contents

		PAGE
FOREWORD	. . . .	vii
INTRODUCTION	. . . . . .	ix
CHAPT.		
I	ALDERSHOT TO CULLY	1
II	OUR BLOODING AT "112"	12
III	ARTILLERY PARK	22
IV	TANK ALLEY	25
V	THROUGH THE BOCAGE	31
VI	ON TO LAIGLE	38
VII	THE GREAT "SWAN"	42
VIII	THE BULL DIVERTS	56
IX	WINDMILLS AND CHURCH SPIRES . . .	60
X	NO TURKEYS FOR CHRISTMAS . . .	72
XI	INTERMISSION	88
XII	OVER THE RHINE	99
XIII	TO THE BANKS OF THE ELBE . . .	105
XIV	ONE MORE RIVER TO CROSS . . .	116
EPILOGUE	. . . .	122
MAP: NORTH-WEST EUROPE	. , , ,	at end

Introduction

THIS is intended to be the story of a company of The Rifle Brigade in the 11th Armoured Division from D Day to VE Day. In it I have tried to give an impression of the sort of life we led and of our sentiments during it. I hope and think that this must be a typical story of any fighting unit in the British Liberation Army. Nearly all the characters in the story were honest-to-goodness Cockneys, whose superb sense of humour remained supreme throughout even the darkest moments, and I hope that I have managed to illustrate this in some of the incidents I have recorded.

We were, with few exceptions, composed entirely of civilians and Territorials and, as I write this, some have already returned to their peace-time occupations and the remainder will follow. For a period of six years many of us gave up our civilian jobs to take up arms for a cause which we believed to be right, and during which we probably saw more of human sentiment and life than we would ever have seen had the war not occurred.

I have been greatly helped in writing this story by people who were constantly at my side during the period covered by this book. Kingsmill supplied the information for the periods during which for some reason I was not present, and Roberts has put in endless work on the preparation of maps and sketches. Bishop wrote his impressions on Brussels, and Cross spent countless hours on his typewriter hammering out the script.

Finally, none of this could have been achieved without the part played by all the characters represented in this story. To them I owe a debt which can never be repaid and gratitude which I can never adequately express.

NOEL BELL

CHAPTER I

ALDERSHOT TO CULLY

ROUSE ! The sound of the bugle drifted across the parade ground. Another day was starting—just another day.

In came the Orderly Sergeant, followed diminutively by the Orderly Corporal, demanding "Any sick ?" Better get up, wash, shave, stack your kit. Just another day.

It was the 6th of June.

Breakfast, as usual—and back to the barrack rooms. Then somebody said, "We've landed in France !" Silence—the silence of doubt, incredulity, amazement. Then, "Where did you hear ?" "Are you sure ?" Strange we should have been surprised when we had been waiting for years to hear this news. Strange it should cause doubt, when we ourselves were toeing the line awaiting the signal shot. Certainly the air activity that morning had been tremendous.

We found a radio and listened; and at a quarter to ten General Eisenhower spoke, and we knew for ourselves. At last it had come ! The Allied armies, with great air support, had landed at many points along the Normandy coast, between the Orne and the Vire.

And it was Battalion Sports Day. We envisaged a speedy cancellation of our athletics and away to the battle; but no, we were to emulate Drake and finish the game before taking up our arms.

It was a warm day, but the near-cloudless sky held not the sun alone. Allied aircraft, with their freshly painted stripes of recognition, shared it—indeed, they overfilled it. It was a wonderful sight to watch them. It filled us with awe, and it filled us with confidence.

The sports went off smoothly. A happy day, and a happier climax to our many years in England. At one o'clock, under the shade of the grandstand, and while we ate our picnic lunches, we listened to the news and heard the report that the Prime Minister had, that morning, made to the House of Commons. That heartened us and renewed our confidence. As we returned to barracks we felt excited, exhilarated. On everybody's lips was the question, "When do we leave ?"

That evening we watched the gliders fly softly overhead. They seemed unending as the fighters had been by day; it was an inspiring sight. As we gazed upwards, helped on, no doubt, with the knowledge that we should soon be with them, I think many a silent prayer went up from us for those boys. At nine o'clock we listened to the King's broadcast, and after much discussion retired to bed—but not immediately to slumber. To ponder over the past; to wonder over the future; to reminisce; to try and foresee and, finally, to sleep.

It was not till the next day that we had our move orders. We were to be prepared to leave at 0530 hrs. the following morning, for our marshalling area. All the waterproofing of vehicles and equipment, which had taken so many arduous days, had been completed the previous week, and all the trucks were part-loaded. We spent the day completing our loading, and when we had finished we wondered if there would be room for us on our armoured steeds at all. Up to the canvas roofs our kit was stacked—most of the personal kit and certain other items being contained in an almighty waterproof sheet, which had been placed on the empty floor of the truck, and on to which all this equipment had been piled. Then the ends were brought up and gathered together at the top, and securely tied, to form a huge bag. It looked rather grotesque sitting there, taking up well over half the back of the truck. All boxes and tins, whether inside this bag or not, were sealed with asbestos compound—a sticky, evil-smelling, plastercine-like material. The wireless sets on the command vehicles were tied up like Christmas presents in their special bags, to prevent the all-corroding sea-water's admittance. The truck looked like an ogress's well-filled shopping basket.

And somehow, we were still to get on.

That evening we each drew two hundred francs in the new Liberation notes, and a little handbook entitled "France." On the front cover of this was a picture of the Arc de Triomphe. It made us think, that picture. We wondered if and when we should ever see Paris. It seemed such a long way from the Normandy beaches—such a very long way!

The 8th of June dawned fair, but we were up long before daybreak came. We packed our bedding, completed our toilet and breakfasted, and were ready to move in our trucks at 0515 hrs., as ordered. It was, however, another hour before we finally pulled out of the barracks on the first stage of our great journey. Those who were "home details," and those who were to come over with the rear party, bade us farewell as we drove out through the main gates. There was a sea of faces, uplifted, as we turned on to the road, but one especially we all remember. It was that of Sergeant-Major Bettles. His entire countenance told us just how much he wished he was coming with us—with "his" "G" Company. But his job was in England, to train more men to reinforce us.

We drove straight down to the main road and headed for London. There was a lot of dust thrown up from the half-tracks, but otherwise it was a pleasant ride sitting on, rather than in, our vehicles. As we approached the metropolis a police escort picked us up and took us through the Greater London area. Many of us passed within shouting distance of our homes. Housewives smiled as they waited in their shopping queues; factory workers cycling to work waved to us encouragingly as we passed by. It all felt rather like 1939 again. Finally, the houses began to thin out and

London was gone. We wondered how long it would be before we saw it again. We knew some of us would never see it again. The Essex countryside was opening up around us, and before we realized it we were in our marshalling area a mile or two from Tilbury.

The first impressions of our camp were not heartening. True, it was to be our home for only a short time, but it seemed so barren, so friendless. Barbed wire had been erected rather half-heartedly around the perimeter, and inside there was a mass of tents and marquees, dotted with an occasional wooden hut. The soil was dusty rather than sandy, and the whole thing was vaguely reminiscent of Rugeley. However, the organization was good and bore no comparison to our material surroundings. We were soon allotted our quarters, seven or eight men to a tent. We settled in.

That evening we were issued with various novelties for our first "fend-for-yourself" hours ashore. We were soon the proud possessors of two "twenty-four hour packs," those little packages which, by dint of their contents of dehydrated porridge, dehydrated meat, some four bars of chocolate and some chewing-gum, together with other assorted oddments, were to keep us "fighting-fit" (sic) for our first forty-eight hours in France. Together with the packs we were issued with a hexamite cooker, on which we were to bring to some form of recognition and, we hoped, also heat the little surprise packets above described. This hexamite cooker consisted of a small foldable metal stand which, when opened out, displayed three legs with (to use a well-loved Army term) a "cut-away portion" in the centre. Into this was placed a hexamite tablet—a circular cake about two inches wide and half an inch deep—which, when ignited by a match, gave a very hot flame. We were also given little tins of water-purifying tablets, each of which contained two small bottles. The first contained tablets to put sufficient taste in the water to kill anything, the second, other tablets to take away the taste of the first. So, finally, like in the old game, we were left with the number we first thought of minus, we hoped, the microlepidoptera. We were also presented with a very fine pair of water wings. Later, the field cashier changed all our remaining English money into French francs, unfortunately not before we were told there was a N.A.A.F.I. in the camp, which only accepted English currency.

Early the following morning the drivers took their vehicles down to the quay, where the final stage of waterproofing was carried out. That completed, loading commenced—a full day's work, which went on until 2100 hrs. Meanwhile, back in the camp area, both spiritual and temporal preparation was being continued for the days ahead. Church services were well attended and gave a renewed feeling of confidence, both in our cause and in ourselves. In the tents men lounged, swotting over their new phrase books, while others repaired to the barber's shop for a Dartmoor trim.

By the time it was evening we were becoming restless. Our journey started, we wanted to get on. A film show which was put on allayed our desires temporarily, but not for long, and it was with a feeling of great relief that, before we retired for the night, we knew that the next day we would embark.

We rose early, packed and had breakfast. Then the whole Battalion formed up and marched off by companies. Nostalgically, we knew that never again would the same Battalion parade as one. We marched out of the camp to a line of waiting trucks which carried us down to the dockside. There, in front of our craft, the United States Liberty ship *Samsit*, we alighted and sat on the quayside and waited. Slowly we embarked, excited to be aboard, yet loath to leave English soil. By ten minutes past midday the ship was loaded, all "G" Company together with "H.Q." Company, elements of other companies, and some Gunners and Sappers.

The bulk of the Company were housed in two holds, Nos. 3 and 4, while the vehicles were in the extreme holds. The holds where we slept were fitted out with hammocks and smelt strongly of meat. We were terribly crowded, the lighting was far from good and, to make matters worse, we were not allowed to smoke below. But otherwise things were not too bad and we soon acclimatized ourselves.

At 1628 hrs. on Saturday, the 10th of June, we cast off. Spirits, temporarily lowered on account of our new quarters, immediately rose and, helped by a fresh breeze blowing up from the estuary, we soon felt once again on top of our form. At six o'clock the engines slowed down, and off Southend we dropped anchor. All evening we lay there, and when we awoke next morning we found we had still not moved. Little transpired that day. A church service was held on the foredeck in the morning. Later, providing an attraction of a different kind, a Rifleman fell from the deck down to the depths of No. 5 hold, but was salvaged unharmed except for a shaking. Meanwhile, in No. 4 hold, two other Riflemen were turning their idle hours to much profit by operating, with considerable skill and much showmanship, a crown and anchor board.

Throughout the day the other ships which were to join us in our convoy assembled in the estuary all around us, and in the afternoon the Commodore who was to command the party came aboard, and we realised with pride that the s.s. *Samsit* was to be the convoy's "flagship."

At a quarter past six next morning we weighed anchor and set sail for France. The day was warm, the sea calm. Our panorama was filled with troopships, and here and there could be seen an escorting destroyer. As we approached the Straits some of the destroyers raced ahead and laid a smoke-screen that was both impressive and effective, through which in due course we passed. We received orders to lie face downwards on the decks with our steel helmets on, and in that rather uncomfortable and undignified position we came within range of our first German guns. However, all passed without incident; we were neither shelled nor attacked from either sea or air; and it was with much relief, and not a little creaking of bones, that the order to "stand down" was received. It was not till later that we heard that the Navy had laid a fake smoke-screen, some hours before our arrival, to which the enemy gunners in the Calais area had given no little attention.

By the time we were through "Bomb Alley" it was afternoon, and most of us were sunning ourselves on the decks. The Channel was like a mill-pond as we idly watched the English coast go by, enthusiasts pointing out the towns and villages they thought they recognized, for we were still very close inshore. It was not till early evening that we finally turned south and headed straight for France.

At last, for it seemed a long day, night came upon us. Except for the sound of distant depth-charging just before midnight, everything seemed very still. Those of us who were on watch that night found ourselves, very literally, between two fires. We could see the conflagrations on the French coast, and in the opposite direction we saw the fires started by German planes over Portsmouth way. At four o'clock in the morning a glider bomb fell between us and the next ship, but many knew nothing about it, for the atmosphere down in the holds was oppressive and the men slept heavily. The incident caused no damage to the ships and we suffered no casualties, but "action stations" was sounded twenty minutes later, and lasted for two hours until our air cover arrived. Meanwhile, at six o'clock we had come to a standstill, but only for ten minutes, and it was not till eight o'clock that we finally dropped anchor off the beaches of Normandy.

We looked about us. Everywhere there were ships, little and big. Troop transports and landing-craft of all types intermingled in the amazing picture before our eyes. The water was alive with the Royal Navy and the Merchant Marine. From many ships flew barrage balloons, giving a homely and friendly touch to a foreign and bloody shore. On the coast itself, between the shattered farmhouses and wrecked cafes, little figures were teeming, each one busy about his individual and vital work. We could not have hidden, had we tried, our amazement at the realization of how much planning had gone into this operation. We knew now why we had waited four years to come back to France.

Much of the morning had passed while we watched and waited before a landing-craft arrived to take off our first batch of men and vehicles. There was an ugly shell-hole through her bridge. Unloading commenced, and much confusion ensued until a party of stevedores from the Royal Engineers came aboard and evolved a system. Soon it was in full motion. Our half-tracks, fully loaded, swung like marionettes in a puppet show as they were lifted out of the holds and placed, so surprisingly gently, on the deck of the landing-craft. As each truck was transferred, so its crew clambered down a rope ladder on the ship's side and joined it. Just before two o'clock the first load left, with 10 Platoon's vehicles and crews complete, with Kenneth Chabot in command. Owing to tides, however, they were not allowed to land until four o'clock, but were still the first troops of the Company ashore. The second load, consisting of 11 and 12 Platoons, followed in like manner. The carriers came off last.

There was more deck space in our landing-craft than we had realized, but the vehicles were nose to tail and had their sides nearly touching, so we were well crowded. The sea was choppier now, or perhaps it was the effect of being in a smaller craft. As we pulled away from the *Samsit* it began to rain lightly, but the spray was quite heavy as we gathered speed and it passed practically unnoticed. We were feeling excited—very excited ! We passed other transports still awaiting disembarkation, and one hospital ship going back to Blighty. Blighty ! It seemed a long way away now.

We looked ahead of us. The coastline became more distinct as we approached and we perceived there were sand-dunes at the top of the beach in front of the village. Behind the latter the ground rose steadily to form a low ridge which blotted from view the country beyond. Estimation of distance over water is always deceptive, and we found we had farther to go than we had imagined; but finally, anticipation gave way to reality. The bottom of the craft grated against the shingle—it shuddered, then came to a standstill. The ramp went down. Before us lay Courseulles-sur-Mer. We were there.

The trucks drove off into the water, but the pilot had found a place that gave us, as near as possible, a dry landing, and the sea did not encroach inside the vehicles to any extent. A naval officer was saying, "Keep her revving; don't get stuck there." We kept her revving. The engine hiccoughed, and we felt the track make the gradient of the beach. We emerged. Water dripped off the suspensions. The sand, soft as it was, felt firm and good after our seventy-two hours afloat. A military policeman was pointing where to go. We turned left and down along the beach, running parallel to the sea. The barbed wire hung in torn shreds, and the sand-dunes were pocked with shell-holes and slit trenches. On a corner where we turned right, down a track, there was a little wooden cross, made out of a "compo" box, inscribed "A Canadian soldier lies here." That was all. No name, no regiment, no date. Momentarily I thought of the majesty of the Unknown Warrior's tomb in Westminster Abbey, then I looked again at that cross. We moved on.

A hundred yards down the track we halted, and the drivers did their first stage—emergency—de-waterproofing. Here, too, we married up with the first party ashore and, after a few minutes, we lumbered on over the uneven ground into the village. Beyond it we passed through a German minefield, still wired off, and marked with the skull and crossbones sign. We began to climb the ridge. Half-way up, to our left, there was a crashed American fighter. Just past this, on the other side of the road, were three British graves in a line, with a khaki cap hung over each of the uprights of the crosses. As we gained the top of the ridge we turned to have a final look at the sea. It was early evening now and the rain had ceased. The sun was shining on the sea and ships, and high above it glistened on the blimps.

We passed the summit, and the rolling Normandy countryside opened out before us. Everywhere there were cornfields, all gently waving in the summer breeze. Infantry were marching up the sides of the road in single file, sweat pouring off their faces as they laboured under their heavy loads of packs, rifles and shovels. They turned their red faces to the side as we passed in a vain effort to keep the swirling dust, sucked up by our half-tracks, out of their eyes. We passed a farm. An aged Norman, clad in old black trousers and a faded blue dungaree jacket, stood by the gate, pipe in mouth, and a white stubble on his chin. He did not smile; only a dog barked. Then we saw his broken farmhouse, and we realized why he had not waved.

Our route took us through a little town called Creully. As we approached it we saw a small procession coming down the road towards us—some score of people, with a young couple leading. Everybody seemed to be carrying a bouquet. It was a bridal procession. The newly-weds laughed up at us as we passed. They were the first ones to do so since we had landed. We turned left at Creully, and as we emerged from the town we heard a machine gun chattering across the hills in the distance. We continued to Lantheuil, a little village with narrow streets and a very sharp turn in the centre. The vehicles negotiated it with difficulty, and a short way outside the village we pulled into a field and halted. We were told we would spend the night there, and immediately dug in. It seemed rather like a scheme. We had nearly finished our slit trenches when the order came, so typically, to move on to Cully, the next village. We boarded our trucks and turned off down the road.

Cully transpired to be not an unpleasant place, in the usual Norman style—a little austere, but not badly knocked about. Most of the farmhouses, which bore a certain vague resemblance to Cotswold design, were enclosed within high stone walls. Some of the houses had front gardens, bright with summer flowers. We found that attractive to our tired, dust-ridden eyes. The church tower, standing at the far end of the village, conformed to pattern and had a gaping shell hole through it, to render it useless as a gunner's observation post.

Our little convoy turned into a farm, proceeded through the courtyard and into the orchard beyond. We drove right round the orchard, keeping to the sides. As our vehicles drove under the fruit trees a shower of young, unripened apples cascaded down upon us, the result of the impact of the turret on the low branches. We halted, parked the trucks in some form of order along the hedge, dug in again, and put up camouflage. The carriers arrived later, and by the time they were in it was nearly dark. We made our beds close by our slit trenches, and put our rifles, steel helmets and equipment beside them; we were new to the game and wished to take no chances, although the nearest Boche was reported over three miles away.

We took off our jackets and boots and slid in between our blankets. The evening was still, and the air smelt fresh and good. We had been in bed but a few minutes, when it started. The whole sky appeared to become a mass of red tracer and searchlights. The Luftwaffe was out to pay its nightly visit to the beaches.

We could not see any of the planes, for it was dark now, and none seemed to get entangled in the beams of the searchlights; but the noise was terrific. Bofors and, here and there, heavy ack-ack guns were blasting away. Above it all there was the undulating drone of the Boche planes. The sky, torn by tracer and starred with bursting shells, looked like a fantastic firework display. Then it faded as quickly as it had come, after a parting belt from one of the Bren guns. Quiet again, and sleep. The memorable 13th of June was drawing to a close.

The following morning we had the unusual experience of being roused at 0530 hrs. by the Commanding Officer. The night had passed without incident, and it was difficult with the return of the daylight not to believe we were not just on another scheme. First thought was breakfast, for we were very hungry. Happily, we had no need to use the twenty-four hour packs, neither the hexamite cookers. We opened up a compo pack and cooked our meal on our No. 2 cooker, a much more civilized affair, with a petrol burner. We even had no need to use our water-purifying tablets, neat as they were, for a good supply of drinking water was found nearby. The final party arrived shortly after we had finished, having spent the night on a landing-craft and reporting it none too pleasant. They had experienced the air activity which we had witnessed. With them they brought the echelon. The whole Battalion was now altogether, harboured in the orchard.

We did not know how long we had before we were called into battle, and no time was wasted, in consequence, of de-waterproofing all our equipment and that part of the engines which had not been done the previous day. A huge dump of the waterproof fabric, together with the other materials we had used, was made at the far end of the orchard. It was a veritable mound. Beside it was a lesser pile, where our water-wings were deposited, except by those pessimists who foresaw many a river crossing in leaky assault boats. That job completed, the trucks were forthwith reloaded for battle. Without the all-embracing shroud of waterproofing materials, we found there was much more room in the vehicles, and although we were well crowded we at least could sit *in* them at last and get ourselves under the level of the armour plating—a problem to which all of us gave much thought.

The following morning we were awakened sharply by the sound of machine-gun fire. We gained consciousness and leapt into our slits in one and the same moment. Never was such speed witnessed. It transpired that Michael Lane, seeing a plane flying over the camp, had blazed away with all he had. A pity—it was a Spitfire!

We resumed our work that day where we had left off the night before, until we felt confident that the stage was set when the call came. Wireless batteries that had become flat during the crossing and subsequent travels were recharged on our chore-horses, and the pulsating rhythm of the engines impinged upon our eardrums throughout the day. Towards evening we watched a fair-sized force of Bostons fly over in formation to bomb a target somewhere west of Caen. It gave us an enormous thrill to see them, and we gazed till our eyes were sore. One was caught in the flak and, after some grotesque aerobatics, came down in flames to send up, as it hit the ground, that macabre mushroom of dark-coloured smoke which we were soon to know so well.

Two days later we received orders to move to our new location on the other side of the village, where we were to join our friends of the 3rd Royal Tank Regiment, for it was not our lot to fight as a Battalion, but each motor company was attached to an armoured regiment, and under its command, to form a "regimental group." We could not, however, have wished for better comrades and, as we had happily discovered in England, "G" Company and 3rd Royal Tank Regiment were a perfect combination in every respect.

It was Derby day, and neither fire nor brimstone, let alone a mere invasion, would prevent us having a sweepstake. We had time to sell the tickets and listen to the radio broadcast before we left. Gobbett, who had drawn Ocean Swell in the draw, won the first prize and was presented accordingly with 730 francs.

We found our new location yet another orchard, but a pleasanter one, and it gave more shade. There was a good-sized stream running through the length of the next field, which was also an asset. We settled in, dug fresh trenches, camouflaged up and erected our tarpaulins between the trucks and the trees to provide shelter. "Tusky" Blackburne joined us with his clutter of anti-tank guns, and we began to feel quite a composite battle group. Unfortunately, however, having no tanks at which to shoot, he persisted in firing his rifle at stray pigeons from time to time, which caused no little alarm, as we were extremely sniper-conscious.

Days passed. The young expeditionary force was getting organized. Mail was arriving daily, also papers, which were only two days old, and that seemed very reasonable. We also had our own radio programme, to which we could listen, which had been operating since D+1; and even "G" Company boasted its own news-sheet. A sports day was arranged. The weather could not have been better, and a great programme was laid on of humorous as well as the more conventional athletic events. At the conclusion, the "Duchess of Cully," a disguise which fooled many, graciously gave away the prizes.

Much as we were enjoying ourselves, for the novelty of the whole thing had not yet worn off, we began to wonder when we would be ordered to battle—we had landed over a week ago now. We learned in due course that the bad weather in the channel was delaying operations, owing to the time taken to off-load the vital supplies. We knew full well our role; we had practised it so many times on the bare wolds of Yorkshire. The infantry were to make a breach in the defences that hemmed in the bridgehead, and we, the armoured columns, were to exploit that breach and break out with all possible speed as far as we could go. We were well posted with information, both through the Army channels and, to a lesser extent, by the B.B.C., and we devoured all the bulletins with relish.

In a general sense the daily routine became fairly regular. There were many conferences between the 3rd R.T.R. and ourselves as to future tactics, especially with regard as to how to negotiate the Bocage. This Bocage was the name given to that type of country, so common in Normandy, where sunken roads were accompanied by a double hedge on either side, with a ditch running between the twin hedges. This made not only an excellent natural tank obstacle and, if the tanks were on the road, confined them to it, thus preventing them from manœuvring on to the country on either side, but also gave first-class cover to the enemy who, whether armed with a machine gun or a panzer-faust, could cause untold damage to an armoured column whilst remaining to a very large extent unobserved. After much discussion, drills were finally decided for this and other tactical problems.

Meanwhile, with the weather improving, we bathed in the stream and did our first "active service" washing, great care being taken to ensure our "whites" were not visible from the air whilst they were drying. Walks were now organized, for we were getting little exercise. It was impossible for us to go far, for obvious reasons, but the Company, by platoons, made a trip to Coulombs, the next village to the west, and back, visiting Cully church and, by way of contrast, a knocked-out German 88 mm. gun on the route.

Our nights were still very noisy, for if, for once, the German planes decided not to pay their nightly visit to the beaches, it was a safe bet that there would be some infantry attack going in which needed full artillery support; and the 7.2 guns shared Cully with us. Many nights we had both ack-ack and field artillery to lull us to sleep, but it was all good training for the sound of battle yet to come.

On one occasion H.M.S. *Rodney* supported an attack, and her 16-in. shells whistled over our heads for a seemingly unending period to crash loudly, though distantly, in the country beyond.

It was now June the 23rd, and we had been ten days in France. That day we acquired many .50 Brownings, from the 3rd R.T.R., who found them superfluous on their Shermans. We mounted them on our trucks and carriers and even on our scout car. They certainly improved the visual aggressiveness of our vehicles, though from a tactical point of view their field of fire was small in many cases, being limited owing to the inadequacy and, in some cases, the bad placing of the gun mountings. They gave us, nevertheless, much confidence in our "ack-ack" defence.

Kenneth Chabot visited our old friends the 24th Lancers that evening and brought off a most excellent barter by bringing back a complete 19 set, which he had been given in exchange for a tin hat. This set was mounted into "O.2," thus giving both command trucks two 19 sets apiece—a blessing, the full value of which we were not to realize till later. He also returned with much fresh butter and a considerable quantity of Camembert cheeses, which improved our menus enormously and put our compo tinned margarine and processed cheese respectively to shame.

The following day, Sunday, the 24th of June, brought with its sunshine and warmth our orders at last to move into battle. Whilst the final touches were made to the vehicles and equipment, Order Groups persisted throughout the day. We sat under the apple trees in the welcome shade and heard the great plan unfolded before us. The 15th Scottish Division were to make a breach in the enemy's line in the area of Cheux, some miles to the south, and we were to follow through leaving Carpiquet aerodrome to our left, cross the River Odon, seize two pieces of high ground in our stride—Hill 112 and Hill 113—and cut the main road running out of Caen to the south-west, after crossing the River Orne. The marked maps were laid out before us. We looked at them and at each other. The operation was certainly ambitious, for it was expected we would cross the Orne the following night, but we, fresh from our training, green, but full of confidence, believed we could do it. The breakout was on a divisional scale, and all the Battalion would be participating, each motor company with its own armoured regiment.

At five o'clock the Commanding Officer visited us and wished us God-speed in our great endeavour. Spirits were high, and hopes were higher. For years we had waited for this. Our little band of men—"G" Company—a handful of Londoners, had a debt to settle with the Hun, and tomorrow we were going to get our first chance to hit back.

It rained that evening. We undressed, as much as we ever did, and clambered into our blankets. Boots off to-night; last time till God-knew-when. We lay in bed and listened to the raindrops falling from the trees above us on to the tarpaulin. We thought of home. We thought of England. And while the rain kept up its incessant drip, drip, we thought of the morrow. We slept.

CHAPTER II

OUR BLOODING AT "112"

MORNING came. Of necessity we rose early, packed up and pulled out of our orchard on to the track that led down to the main road. The orchard, which had been our home for just over a week, looked strangely bare when the last of the vehicles had moved, and light green patches on the grass showed where our bivouacs had been.

We formed up in line along the track with the tanks in front of us, and halted. It was half-past eight, the time laid down when we would start, but there was no sign of movement. After an hour had passed, we climbed out of our vehicles and walked up and down the column or lay on the grass verges under the high trees that flanked both sides of the lane. In the distance a great artillery barrage was going down in the direction of where our objectives lay.

The morning passed, and it was one o'clock before orders were eventually received to proceed. We turned left on to the main road through Cully and forked left at the far end of the village. At the fork the members of the echelon, who were staying in Cully, smiled and waved their farewells and wished us good luck. It was warm now, and the sun was at its height; all sign of the previous night's rain had disappeared in the heat.

The roads were bad, being pitted with holes, and we jolted along rather uncomfortably. The country was close for the most part, and thick bushes and high trees frequently hid the surrounding fields from our eyes. We passed through Secqueville-en-Bessin and on to Bretteville-l'Orgueilleuse, where we crossed the main road running from Bayeux to Caen. Both villages, but especially the latter one, were badly mauled, and the ruined houses and shops bore silent witness to the heavy fighting and shelling which had taken place there. A knocked-out German self-propelled assault gun lay between two houses in a little alley-way off the road. It was blackened with fire, and one of its tracks hung limp, shattered and useless across the suspension. Gaily-coloured advertisements for Byrrh and Cinzano, painted on the sides of houses, were spattered with mud from near-by shell bursts. Enamelled signs displaying "Boulangerie" and "Boucherie-Charcuterie" hung by a thread from their brackets or from a solitary nail from the front of broken-down shops. And all-pervading, above it all, was the sweet, sickly, repulsive smell of death. Outside the village, destruction was no less apparent, and dead cattle, blown and stinking, lay round the smouldering farms. Truly, the four horsemen of the Apocalypse were riding through Normandy.

Less than a mile from Bretteville the column halted by a level crossing, and a few shells landed nearby. The surrounding cornfields were littered with Canadian dead. The railway had been the enemy's line of defence until that morning. One half-track was ordered off the road into a cornfield on the left to keep the way clear. It had gone only a few yards when it was discovered that the whole area was sown with mines. Indeed, a crippled tank beside us bore testimony. Gingerly the driver started to back the truck on to the road again. All was silence, save for the quiet throb of the engine and the crushing of the cornstalks. It regained the road safely. Another thirty seconds had passed that seemed like a day.

We pulled our truck on to the other side of the road into a yard, which lay at the back of a smouldering, white-painted building. The roof had fallen in, and some of the beams glowed red in the light breeze. In the yard were two knocked-out Canadian Bren-carriers, and a steel helmet lay some ten yards from them with a gaping gash in its side. Just beside us was a human leg, still wearing its German jack-boot. The boot was upraised, and the studs glistened in the sun.

We did not cross over the railway at the level crossing, but turned right and ran alongside it for about a mile before negotiating the rails in an open patch between two woods. The infantry, who were making the breach, were still fighting in front of us, and our speed was therefore largely regulated by their progress. It was early evening now and, leaving the woodland behind us, we came to a piece of flat ground that was quite desolate and barren. Smoke from some burning houses to the left drifted across it slowly, almost wearily, giving it an uncanny dream-like effect.

All around us was the litter of men's kit, water-bottles and respirators, a rifle or two, steel helmets and sets of equipment. Behind us, to our right, a group of men were digging graves for the Canadians who had been killed there in a previous sally. In the distance, to the west, air-bursts were clouding the sky near the horizon. We passed on to more pleasant surroundings and found ourselves driving down a grassy slope between woods on either side. The slope ran down to a little hollow where there were many 25-pdrs. We halted there and made a brew, and received new orders. A dead horse lay by the hedge. The 25-pdrs. were firing for all they were worth, and their muzzle flashes made quick stabs in the fast-falling darkness. We stayed there till about midnight, then continued up the slope out of the hollow to form close laager in a field on the right. Most of us slept in our vehicles where we sat, for it had been a long day, and the psychological reaction of some of the things we had seen brought additional weariness.

The next morning 10 Platoon, together with some "Honey" tanks of the 3rd R.T.R., made a patrol into St. Mavieu, a village a mile to the east, where some snipers had been reported. They found it clear of the enemy, but there was some fighting going on in a wooded area to the south-east. They did not return to us in the laager area, but made a wide sweep round to the left towards Carpiquet reconnoitring the country. Meanwhile, just before midday, the rest of the company set off once again southwards. Cheux was the next locality we encountered, a small Norman town which must have been quite pretty a day or two before. It was an unhappy sight that day. It had been treated like Bretteville, only worse. The church, once, no doubt, a beautiful piece of craftsmanship, had lost its tower, roof, and much of its walls. Most of the buildings were in ruins, some of them still burning. Infantry were still clearing the houses, and some shooting was going on in another part of the town. As we turned a corner, we came across a dead cow lying in the middle of the road, and near it, on the left, was a knocked-out half-track. Two men were sitting in the back huddled forward. They were dead.

We came out of Cheux and struck left over open country, heading south-east. The ground sloped gradually down before us, and it was dotted with woods. 10 Platoon married up with us again, and the tanks, which had bypassed Cheux to the left, also joined up and took the lead, making a screen in front of us, in extended order. The Company were in similar formation. We rolled down the slope. Suddenly a gun spoke; once, twice, and again. Some sparks seemed to fly off one of the leading tanks, and the air was filled with a sound like that of a racing car passing at great speed—a rushing, whirring note. A moment's pause and the tank burst into a mass of flames. Micky said, "Eighty-eights." We were too green to be scared, for we failed to realize the significance of it all. It had not yet registered on our minds that we were in the enemy gunner's sights, and at that moment another armour-piercing shell was being loaded into the breech. It was our first taste of direct enemy action, and it seemed coincidental that the shells were coming our way. We had yet to learn to be afraid. We had yet to learn to respect the German 88 mm. We moved forward a little, then stopped; and moved on again. In such manner, we progressed, while two more tanks fell victims to the guns. We made a sharp left swing to some higher ground, and halted in the area of a farmhouse. The artillery had stopped firing now. The country in front of us fell slowly down to the east, and we could clearly see Carpiquet airfield, still heavily defended by the Germans, some two miles away. The farm was enclosed by a high stone wall, and a disabled "Honey" tank lay along the southern side. One of our boys went to investigate, climbed on to the turret, and peered inside. He jumped down rather quickly, looking sick. We did not have to ask why.

Some small-arms firing started, and a section of carriers, who were up a track on the far side of the farm with 10 Platoon, brought in two prisoners—our first—having killed a third German who had tried to run away. The prisoners struck us by their extreme youth, looking no more than seventeen. One was a huge fellow, with blond hair and blue eyes; a typical Hun. Both appeared intensely arrogant, and we learned they were from an S.S. Hitler Youth battalion.

Our attention was soon distracted, however, by some Typhoons over Carpiquet. They were firing their rockets into the hangars, and it cheered us no end to see them. The presence of the Typhoons, together with the subsequent damage they caused, no doubt accounted for us being left practically undisturbed, for we were in full view of the enemy, and stayed in that spot several hours. Nevertheless, only two or three shells came over, which whistled over our heads and landed in the fields behind us, causing no damage.

Meanwhile, we had received fresh orders, and in the evening we pulled out and withdrew some distance, passing through Divisional H.Q. on the way to the area of St. Mauvieu. It was dark by the time we arrived, and at a crosstracks we met up with the echelon and halted. We were given ten minutes to replenish—a job that usually took half an hour, even in daylight. Petrol and rations had to be drawn, water-cans filled from the trailer, and batteries changed on the wireless sets. During replenishment, orders were given out. Rather an alarming picture was painted of driving down a road, flanked with thick woods, infested with snipers and bazooka men. We were to look out both sides of the truck all the time, as well as front and rear, and to have rifles and grenades ready. Somebody made a joke, and we laughed softly. It was good to laugh again. It seemed so long since we had done so. The orders continued. We were to cross the Odon, form a bridgehead on the far bank, then thrust on to take Hill 112. We moved into the blackness.

When we arrived at the stretch of road, about which we had been warned, nerves were tense; fingers caressed triggers, and exerted slight, impatient pressure on the pins of grenades. It was very still, and the soft, gentle crunching of the gravel beneath the tracks was the only sound that mingled with the whispering of the breeze. Suddenly the column stopped. The leading vehicle had stumbled across a despatch rider from the King's Shropshire Light Infantry. They asked him what he was doing there, and he told them his battalion were down the road in front of us. We breathed more freely, and proceeded a short distance. Then, about two o'clock in the morning, we pulled into an orchard, and the Company formed a very close laager. Sentries were posted. Of a sudden, we were conscious of being shaken. We opened our eyes. It was daybreak, and we had slept for two hours. Trucks were immediately started and we moved on. Down the road we went, through Colleville and Mondrainville, both of which the infantry had entered before us. The usual scenes met our gaze; dead Germans, dead cattle, wrecked and burning houses, and the usual stench accompanied them.

At the bottom of a hill we came to a bridge by a bend. Some Reconnaissance cars were on the bridge. We crossed. It was the

River Odon, and from now on we would have to fight our own way. We were level now with the leading elements of the infantry. This was the break-out. We climbed up the steep, winding hill the other side. Near the top, some five hundred yards from the crest, we stopped, and Company H.Q. pulled into a farmyard on the right-hand side of the road. 10 and 11 Platoons were sent out on a patrol to investigate some wooded area which lay about a thousand yards to our right rear, backing on to the river. The first patrols brought a nil result, and a second effort was ordered, as it was considered certain that there were enemy in that area, and we could not afford to move on with such a threat to our flank. Meanwhile, the carriers had taken up positions hull-down behind a bluff, observing the far side of the river to the west of where we had crossed, and our 3-inch mortars moved down in support of the patrols. This time the patrols met trouble. David Stileman was leading a section of 11 Platoon down a hedge, the remainder of the platoon being some way behind. Without warning, from a strongpoint, disguised as a refuse dump some twenty-five yards ahead, a low angle mortar was fired, which landed on the far side of the hedge, rendering all the men there, casualties. 10 Platoon, who were up on the left, came down to their assistance, and in a fresh outbreak of machine-gun and mortar fire, Michael Lane was wounded, together with several others. Later, Michael died of his wounds. Micky McCrea went down in the scout car in an effort to get things cleared up. As he approached, he was sniped at, and a bullet entered his knee. He was brought back on the scout car, looking very white. The patrol withdrew, and the casualties were evacuated. On arrival back, Sergt. Allwinkle was missing. Happily he showed up some time later, and it transpired that he had been pinned down by Spandau fire, while the rest of the platoon were withdrawing, and it was many hours before he eventually succeeded in making good his exit. Meanwhile, some infantry had arrived opposite Company H.Q., and were digging in in an orchard on the other side of the road. The responsibility of the right flank was handed over to another company, as it was considered vital that we should push on and make ourselves strong on 112.

It was early afternoon now. We climbed aboard our vehicles and, describing a circle in the field in front of us, emerged at the top of the hill by a crossroads. There we passed over diagonally, and continued across country. We were heading due east now, and the village of Baron lay on our left. There was a scrap going on there between the K.S.L.I. and some enemy infantry. As we drew level to the village we swung up right and, leaving an L-shaped wood to our left, started to climb the lower slopes of Hill 112.

We had been told to expect trouble here, for there were a lot of Boche reported in the thick corn which grew waist-high on the slopes, and also in the woods to our left. We ascended with the half-tracks in column and the carriers guarding the flanks. We rumbled over the fields, slowly climbing. The carriers were firing their Brownings into the woods, and suddenly return fire started. Bullets pinged off the sides of the vehicles with monotonous regularity. We made sure our heads were below the level of the armour-plating, while the drivers adjusted their visor-slits to the minimum. Throughout, we continued climbing slowly, so slowly it seemed, up the hill. As we neared the top. Typhoons swept down and fired their rockets into a small wood, by the summit, sending up great columns of dirt. The small-arms firing ceased, and we turned into a square field which was surrounded by tall trees and bushes. There was only one gap, and a steepish bank had to be negotiated before entrance could be gained. The Company aligned itself along the sides of the field, and the anti-tank guns were put into position. This was Hill 112.

The atmosphere was tense, and held that calm which prevails before a storm. Nearly all the half-tracks were ordered to withdraw, as their presence was redundant and, apart from giving away our position unnecessarily, they were easy targets to hit. The ammunition which was required, together with the picks and shovels, was off loaded, and they were sent down the backward slope some six hundred yards behind a concentration of the R.T.R.'s tanks. Back on the hill, the Company dug in. After about half an hour a machine gun opened up, somewhere from the direction of the wood that the Typhoons had previously attacked. It was shortly joined by another, and for some while spasmodic firing continued. It then became apparent that the tempo of the fire was increasing, and soon a great crescendo was reached. The tanks, who were on the left of the field, hull-down behind the ridge, returned the fire, for the Company from their position could not see whence it came. For several minutes the sky was rent with a great flow of tracer in both directions. Just as the climax was achieved, shelling commenced and a further note was also added to the battle-din. It was a diabolical sound, like that of a giant retching, which was repeated several times in quick succession. This was followed by a great whistling, culminating in a devilish scream, as some unknown missiles hurtled down from the sky. It was the German multiple-barrelled rocket mortar, commonly dubbed "Moaning Minnie." To those who have never heard one, the attempted description is quite insufficient. The fearful noise as the rockets leave the barrels is beyond true interpretation on paper. Their purpose was dual, combining both psychological and blast effect, and, like the Stuka, the psychological part was frequently more devastating than the subsequent material damage, which was terrible enough. During this deluge, Brian Oxley-Boyle, commanding 12 Platoon, was shot through the wrist and the leg. After a seemingly interminable time, the crashing ceased. There was another pause that seemed unreal, and was pregnant with expectation, for a counter-attack was the natural complement to such a bombardment. All eyes, never before so watchful, gazed out from the perimeter of the Company defences. After a few minutes infantry were seen advancing from the west. They were making full use of cover and it was difficult to assess their strength. Artillery support was called, and a heartening barrage of 25-pounders showered down on them. Nothing more was seen of the infantry, and there was no counter-attack. It was, however, apparent that the position was quite untenable, in view of our strength, through the hours of darkness, and it was decided to withdraw from the summit. Accordingly, the necessary orders were given and the Company, amid a great fresh outburst of shelling began the descent.

Meanwhile the trucks were ordered back to an orchard that lay on the southern edge of Baron, just behind the L-shaped wood, a distance of some eight hundred yards. The orchard contained several dead cattle, and a farmhouse lying in the north-east corner was completely wrecked. The previous shelling and mortaring had stripped the trees of all their fruit and most of their leaves. Branches, torn off by shell splinters, littered the grass beneath. The grass itself was seared and discoloured with the blast of exploding shells, and was pitted with holes of varying sizes. No sooner had the vehicles been parked there when the first of the Company began to arrive back. Simultaneously, fresh orders were received over the air to get the transport out on the road in the village, facing west. It was apparent there was much confusion, for any orders were hard to get, and they invariably contradicted each other in succession. Nobody seemed to be sure of what was happening, or what the future form was. As the last of the vehicles was being marshalled into column on the road, Brian approached, supported under the arms by two of his section leaders. The parts of his face that were not covered with mud or blood showed through deathly pale. We gave him a shot of brandy from a flask; he coughed. It was nearly dark, and the road was very narrow. The trucks and carriers turned and made their way back through the orchard to the L-shaped wood. As we approached we saw in the place where we were to go a half-track burning. It was one of "H" Company's. On board, ammunition was exploding, and the blazing tyres made vivid circles of flame. We made laager, and attempted to find order out of chaos. Spirits were low, and a great feeling of depression and failure swept through us. There were only two officers left. The task of reorganization went on through the hours of darkness. Few had more than a wink of sleep that night, some none at all. The previous morning seemed another age.

As soon as it was light again we set about digging in. We dug with a will, and by nine o'clock we had trenches of a reasonable depth that would protect us from all but a direct hit. As our trenches deepened, so our confidence returned. A party was detailed to return to the hill to recover the half-track and the two guns which had been ditched the day before. We prepared breakfast. As soon as it was ready the first shells came over, and fell amongst us. Several salvoes were fired, but happily no casualties resulted. Our spirits rose, despite our ruined meal. Then, like a bolt from the blue, came the order that the Company would return to 112. A man nearby said softly: "Oh Christ !" It reflected the feelings of us all. The order had been given, and it was not "for us to reason why." We prepared ourselves and by mid-morning we were ready to start. We climbed on to vehicles, and began the ascent once again. This time the journey was quiet, and we arrived on the summit without a shot being fired. On arrival it was decided that all the vehicles would stay up there this time, but the order was almost immediately countermanded, and again the half-tracks made their way back to the wood that we had left thirty minutes before.

The carriers had been put out on the left flank, with No. 1 Section forward, hull-down behind the crest, and the other two sections behind. The motor platoons and Company H.Q. returned to the square field, and took up their old positions. Just as the last of the trucks had left, shelling and mortaring commenced. All day a continual barrage came down, varying in pitch from time to time. Several times the carriers were blown bodily off the ground by the blast, but, luckily, no direct hits were scored. Typhoons again attacked the wood on the right, and the Company's mortars, working in conjunction with those of "H" Company put down a steady stream of fire on to the enemy position on the forward slope of the hill. Sergt. Hollands, under heavy fire, continued to operate the mortars, until he himself was wounded by shrapnel in the leg.

By his gallant persistence he won himself the Military Medal. Even the grimmest moments have their humour. Naish, leaning against a bank, just above his slit trench, was operating the company wireless off an extension lead from "O.2." and so as to leave his ears more free to pick up sounds of approaching morsels of H.E., he held the headphones in his hand. A shell burst close by, and a piece of shrapnel tore straight through the bakelite parts of the headset, leaving him with the metal band only. Wisely, if a little belatedly, he returned to his hole.

Down at the wood, we parked the vehicles. Some of "H" Company's trucks were already there, and they were running a shuttle service to the top and down again fetching their wounded. Running down the hill came a tank sergeant from the R.T.R. He wanted to know where medical help could be found. His tank had had a direct hit from an 88 mm. His driver was dead, his co-driver had lost both his legs and the gunner had lost his sight. He the commander, standing in the turret, had escaped unharmed. We directed him as best we could and he disappeared towards Baron.

It was not long before mortaring started here, too. A great hail of "Minnies" came over, and one fell just behind one of the trucks. Shrapnel tore a great gash through the armour plate, as though it were tissue paper and some ammunition in the back began to ignite. It was only small arms, and we were able to put it out before the P.I.A.T. bombs which were stacked on the other side of the truck were affected. More mortaring followed and it was decided to move the transport to the western end of the field, about a quarter of a mile away. This was done but it was in vain. We had no sooner arrived when the "Minnies" came over again, falling right in our new position, damaging two more half-tracks. It was apparent, then, that we were under observation and further movement in the immediate area would be useless. Beside where we were parked was a deep sunken lane. We climbed through the hedge, and took the best cover we could down there taking with us an extension lead from the wireless off "O.1." In front of us by about twenty yards, infantry of the K.S.L.I. had dug in, making a second line of defence along the lower slopes of the hill. Over the air, Kenneth Chabot asked for more batteries for his wireless, as the present ones were running flat. The echelon was back at Cully, and such a long journey was out of the question, as they were needed urgently. They would have to be found locally. One man and a driver took a half-track to find what they could. They made for the Battalion H.Q. of the K.S.L.I. that was on the far side of the village. Baron was in a shambles. The shelling and mortaring had finished the destruction that had been started on the previous day. The Signal Sergeant at the K.S.L.I. supplied the necessary batteries, which were duly delivered to Kenneth on the hill-top, and communication was kept open. Upon arrival, it was requested that the drivers might prepare a hot meal and some tea for the men up top, and this was soon under way. The food was packed into heat-resisting containers, and was gratefully received.

A further salvo of "Minnies" came over; the lane was filled with choking acrid smoke, and dust thrown up by the explosion. The back door of "O.1." was open and everything inside was in a chaos from the great blast and the splinters. One of the wireless sets was holed, and blankets were in ribbons. The canvas roof was like a colander.

It was decided to move the trucks. "O.1." would not start and had to be left. They turned right down a track, leaving Baron Church on their left, into the village. Eventually they came to rest again on the northern edge of the village.

Across the other side of Baron, an ammunition truck was blazing, making a great glow in the gathering darkness, which was relieved by vivid flashes as divers types of cartridge, mortar and shell exploded. All around the shelling and mortaring never ceased. The barrage seemed eternal. It began to rain.

Meanwhile, life with the remainder of the Company on "Hill 112" was very far from pleasant. All day long we had waited with every nerve alert for the expected counter-attack, while shells and "Minnies" rained down on us. No. 3 Section of 9 Platoon had been moved to the right flank of the position, and was forward, observing the village of Esquay beneath them. Later, about six o'clock, 10 and

12 Platoons advanced over the crest of the hill, and took up positions on the forward slope, and dug in. Shells, however, exploding in the trees above them evinced the futility of slit-trenches without coverings, as the splinters fell straight into them. In consequence, 10 Platoon pushed out, to the right and 12 Platoon to the left, until they were in the open ground on either side of the wood. There they began to dig in again.

At last light, some eight tanks, reported as Tigers, though not confirmed as such, together with something over 150 infantry, were observed advancing from the west towards the Company positions, by No. 3 Section. Very lights were going up and machine-gunning broke out. The long-awaited counter-attack for which we had waited all day, was coming in at last. Strange as it may seem, there was a certain relieving of tension, for anything was better than that perpetual suspense, not knowing when or whence the attack would come. Now it was coming in, we knew where we stood. Artillery support was again enlisted, and within a matter of minutes, for time was urgent, a devastating barrage was brought to bear on to the advancing infantry. For nearly a quarter of an hour the boot was on the other foot; the gunners succeeded in wreaking complete havoc on the enemy on the ground. The tanks finding their ground support virtually liquidated, withdrew, together with what remained of the infantry, and, with darkness now complete, we awaited our next call to action. Meanwhile, 10 and 12 Platoons, forward on the slope were still observing to the south. There was a wire fence running across their front, about a hundred yards distant, the posts of which were spaced about ten yards apart. In the darkness, as their watchful eyes gazed down through the wires, the posts seemed to take human form, wore German helmets, and carried rifles, according to more than one observer. "So full of shapes is fancy."

Just over an hour before dawn we were again ordered to withdraw. With most of the vehicles already gone, it was once more a case of climbing on to anything that moved. Through the night we made our way back to an area south-west of Norrey-en-Bessin, about four miles away, where transport and men joined up again. By the time the reunion was complete daylight had broken. Even God never knew how good it was for us to see the sun again. The area where we found ourselves as daylight returned was a flattish piece of country, the ground churned up by previous armoured vehicles, and the hedges betrammelled. To the south of us we could discern the remains of Cheux, that unhappy village. We formed a column on the road, and moved off northwards. After about a mile and a half, we came to a small plateau, where we left the road, and pulled in to the open ground on the right. This was to be our laager area while we reorganized. The Company transport was formed into a single column, and we dug in beside our own vehicles. The scene around us was not uplifting, for it was here, soon after D Day that the Canadians had fought a tough engagement in the initial and abortive break-out attempt. Several knocked out Mark IV's lay about, suspension-deep in the cornfields. Here and there, half hidden by the tall, ripening cornstalks, lay a dead soldier, whose blackened face gazed unseeingly towards the sky. Some were in khaki; others in field grey.

For us, Hill 112 was over. It was the 30th of June. As we sat back while stronger formations than ours tried, in their turn, to achieve the supremacy of its summit, we wondered if all warfare was like this.

In the weeks that followed, first Briton, then German held the summit; but it proved to be a virtually untenable position for any time. It was not till all Caen had been cleared, and the first signs of what was to become the Falaise pocket had made themselves apparent, did the Boche finally pull out. But that is another story.

CHAPTER III

ARTILLERY PARK

OUR time at Norrey was spent licking our wounds from Hill 112, and trying to take stock of our freshly gained experience. I don't think any troops could have had a sterner initiation into the unpleasantness of battle than we had on that legendary hill. But two things were firm in all our minds. Our long and often tedious years of training in England had been well worth-while, and it was going even more in future to stand us in good stead. The other thing was—and this was by far the more important—that no matter what troubles, dangers and difficulties lay ahead of us, nothing would dampen the Company spirit built up by toil and laughter during our years in England. The "Ikes" had set out to do a job, and there was nothing that Germany could produce would ever stop them.

We were still grouped with the 3rd R.T.R., and we spent four days dispersed in the fields, with nothing very much to worry us. The occasional shell came over but apart from damaging one of our 6-pdrs. and perforating washing hanging out to dry, no harm came to us. The greatest problem was sorting out and checking kit and stores. We had lost a great amount on Hill 112, and we were to learn later that the more seasoned a campaigner one becomes, the less kit one loses.

On the 7th of July we heard that we were going to take over from the 2nd Bn. King's Royal Rifle Corps, who were sitting in a counter-attack role north of Cheux. I reconnoitred our Company area in the afternoon, and the prospects of this new job appeared, on the face of it, fairly peaceful. I arrived back early evening and gave out orders for the move, which was to take place the next day, and had just about finished giving out the enemy information paragraph when a distant throb of aeroplane engines filled the skies. Looking up, we saw approaching a great black cloud of R.A.F. "heavies" on their way to bomb Caen, prior to the Canadians launching their attack on this old Normandy town, so vital to us for the success of future operations. Order group was automatically suspended while we watched the amazing spectacle of the seemingly endless stream of bombers go in to drop their loads. Anti-aircraft fire, which came up quite strongly at first, was soon smothered and great fires began lighting the sky. Dusk was approaching as the last bomber turned and started off for home, and we envied the crews who would soon be sitting down to a good meal in England. But no one begrudged them it—they had given us a first-class show, which made morale soar. Order group was resumed and details were tied up for our move to Artillery Park, the significance of which name will be seen shortly.

Our reorganization was far from complete when we left Norrey. So far only vehicle and equipment problems had been settled and there still remained the reshuffling of personnel to fill vacancies caused by casualties. At one time it seemed we might lose some of the old members of the Company to supply other companies' needs, but this was largely averted. A new commanding officer, arrived in the person of Tony Hunter from the 60th Rifles, bringing youth to the helm as well as experience gained in the Middle East. Philip May joined the Company and lived with "O.2." His stay with us was short, but during that time he learnt a great deal from the "Basher" in the art of eating enormous meals and making endless brews, which left a lasting impression of "G" Company on his mind.

Our positions were on the side of a hill and we used to man these fully at night and in the morning withdraw to a cornfield in the valley. Operational Company H.Q., however, used to remain on the hill all the time, mainly because we had moved in to a very well bulldozed pit, made by the Light Anti-Aircraft Regiment, and if we had moved out for a minute, they would quickly have retaken it. We rehearsed our counter-attack role, which appeared rather remote and caused a certain amount of umbrage to be taken by the forward troops, as movements in their area brought down a hail of shells and mortar bombs. Nothing of great importance was done during our stay here. Our area had been heavily fought over, and a few dead Germans were found in some of the many slit trenches and dugouts. By far the most unpleasant thing, though, was the presence of dead cattle and the appalling stench of them. We minimized this to a great extent by borrowing a bulldozer from the 3rd R.T.R. and covering them with earth. The bulldozers at this time were in great demand and buried dozens of animals daily.

A truck was run daily to Bayeux to buy butter, cheese and cream for us all. There was a tremendous glut of these commodities in Normandy and if one didn't stop to think, it made one rather doubt all the stories of famine in occupied Europe so prominently featured in the press during the past few years. However, we were to find all the way along that people who lived in the country had very little to complain of in the case of food.

The many knocked-out German tanks in the area were used to good effect to show that our P.I.A.Ts. would very definitely go through them, and although the circumstances never actually arose, it was always comforting to know that in a tight corner we had something which could at any rate knock out a Mark IV German tank.

The "Q" side of the Company here produced our first home-made showers, consisting of perforated jerricans suspended from a horizontal bar and operated by means of pulling a string. In the meantime the cooks worked valiantly with their hydras to maintain the supply of hot water. The whole venture was a great success and was repeated many times afterwards. On the operational side the only shots fired by us during this period were at aircraft, hostile and friendly alike. German planes used to dive out of the clouds and try and catch our air O.Ps. unawares. A hail of fire from all weapons used to greet them, which unfortunately generally became more intense when the pursuing Spitfires arrived on the scene. However, we never actually shot down one of our own aircraft, although we must have given the pilots very many uncomfortable moments. We were still very inexperienced at aircraft recognition, and unless one happened to be in a position where one could observe the actions of the Company Sergeant-Major, it was generally all over before one had time to know whether the aircraft was friendly or hostile. Anyway, the chances of being hit by falling fragments of anti-aircraft shells were far greater than from anything coming out of the aeroplane.

I have nearly reached the end of this chapter, and have so far not touched on the significance of the title of it. We had anticipated comparative peace and quiet in this area, and the chances of our counter-attack role ever having to be undertaken were extremely small. So all looked set for hours of uninterrupted sleep whenever we felt inclined.

However, we were rudely brought to our senses very shortly after our arrival here by artillery reconnaissance parties and by the sight of crews of sweating gunners digging the most gigantic pits. Guns began to arrive in ever-increasing numbers, and the gunners showed signs of having every intention of giving a demonstration of the vast Allied shell superiority over the Germans. The early arrivals did not exceed a calibre of 105 mm. but more was to come, and our fears were realized when the really enormous gunpits began to be filled by equally enormous guns; 7.2 inch and 155 mm. guns then began displaying their superiority in noise and blast over their small brothers, the 25-pdrs. and the mediums.

Night and day this inferno went on, swelling to a mighty crescendo at the end of our stay, when the 15th Scottish Division went through us to battle beyond. The noise that night was terrific, but despite the discomfort of having to listen to it, it was most satisfactory to know that the Germans were at the sharp end of it and were suffering far greater discomfort than we were.

Prior to this attack, a searchlight appeared in our lines, which we viewed at first with a good deal of suspicion and grave misgivings. This searchlight was to produce artificial moonlight for the advancing infantry, and we felt sure something must hit back at it, and, as always happened, would register on us and miss the artificial moon. However, nothing happened, and our previously hostile attitude to the searchlight crew next morning turned to a more congratulatory one.

Artillery Park, far from being a rest cure, had been rather an inoculation for the noise of war, which took extremely well. However, in spite of it all, much had been achieved, spirits were high, and we were once again ready for the tasks which lay ahead of us.

CHAPTER IV

TANK ALLEY

EARLY in the morning of the 16th of July, we left Artillery Park and moved back to some pleasant cornfields near our old haunt, Cully, the whole battalion being concentrated in this area prior to our next venture. A very well attended service was held in the open, and the remainder of the day was spent checking over our supplies and getting what rest we could. As dusk was falling we moved a few miles to join the 3rd R.T.R., with whom once again we were to be grouped in the coming battle, the plans of which were still veiled in secrecy. Shortly after joining them, German aircraft came over and took many flashlight photographs, but as it turned out afterwards, did not get very many clues from them as to the whereabouts of the 11th Armoured Division.

It was close on midnight when we set off, nose to tail, in almost pitch darkness. Most of our movement was along tracks, and the fact that the route was not clearly marked, coupled with the darkness and the great volumes of dust thrown up by the unending columns of armoured fighting vehicles, made the going very difficult. Kenneth Chabot had gone on ahead as a harbour party, and it was with very great relief that we at last met him waiting for us early next morning near Beuville.

We settled into an orchard, and, as we still hoped that the enemy had no idea of our future intentions, great pains were taken to camouflage ourselves. Everyone was very tired after the night drive, and after a quick breakfast I ordered that all would bed down till four o'clock in the afternoon.

While the Company slept I was briefed by Colonel Silvertop of the 3rd R.T.R. for the forthcoming "tank alley" operation, the plan of which was roughly as follows :—

There was to be a great armoured steamroller drive to the east of Caen across the plain towards Falaise. This was to be undertaken by the 11th Armoured, Guards Armoured, and 7th Armoured Divisions in that order following one behind the other in the initial stages of the proposed breakthrough. At the same time, the Canadians were to strike south from Caen, and further over to the east a British infantry division was also going to push south. Between these two infantry drives, there was an alley, down which the armoured brigades of the three Armoured Divisions were going to move. A vast artillery programme had been laid on and the whole operation was to be preceded by heavy and fragmentation bombing on a scale hitherto unknown in such operations.

In the lead of the whole operation were the 3rd R.T.R., and "G" Company, and the formation of our group was two squadrons of tanks in line abreast, followed by a line of flail tanks and the carriers of 9 Platoon. After them came the headquarters vehicles of the group, my command vehicle alongside Colonel Silvertop's tank, together with the Assault Engineers Churchill tanks. The last line consisted of the remainder of the Company and the Royal Horse Artillery's self-propelled guns. The whole formed a square, with the third squadron of the R.T.R. split into two, one-half being on each flank of the square. This formation was to be the same in every regimental group. After the preliminary air and artillery bombardment, we were to move down the alley, following close on a creeping barrage from 25-pdrs. No final objective was fixed, but the really optimistic "higher ups" hoped we might get to Falaise.

The Company was roused at four o'clock, and I gave out orders to the order group and then briefed the Company as a whole. All were greatly impressed by the details I was able to disclose, and we felt sure that we would very soon be making headlines for the papers.

We next set to work camouflaging our vehicles. Very nearly the whole terrain across which we were going to advance consisted of cornfields, and so we tied on bundles of corn all over the vehicles, and this turned out later to be most effective. The only danger of it was that an incendiary or tracer bullet might set it alight and cause the vehicle to catch fire, but, weighing everything up, this seemed to be a risk worth taking.

While all this was going on, the colour sergeant arrived—a most welcome visitor to our orchard, bringing with him, as well as supplies of war, our N.A.A.F.I. rations and a bottle of English beer for each of us. Most of the latter was consumed hastily, many being unwilling to take a chance on their bottles, or they themselves, coming through the battle, and English beer by no means grew on trees in Normandy. Cider had been all we could get to drink, and this upset so many people's stomachs that its first immediate popularity very soon subsided.

Darkness fell and we emerged from our day camouflage to start on the final trek to our concentration area just north of Ranville. This was an even more unpleasant drive than the previous night, as in addition to the dark and dust, we this time had shelling added to the menu. However, no one was hit and we eventually arrived at our destination just before dawn broke. Various vehicles went the wrong way, but they were mostly retrieved and the Company was almost complete, but very tired, by the time H Hour came. Kenneth Chabot was still sorting everyone out when I went with Colonel Silvertop in a scout car to reconnoitre the way to the start line. Just to make things a little more complicated, the 51st Highland Division had laid a minefield, through which gaps had to be made before we could get through.

Before we all moved forward to form up on this lovely sunny summer's morning, of 18th July, we were treated to a superb air pageant by the R.A.F., who appeared to be bombing everything within sight.

Then, over the air came the orders to crack off. All reached their appointed places in the formation except one carrier, which was blown up on one of our own mines. We waited ready to go forward for seemingly interminable minutes. The roar of artillery was terrific on either flank, and a small percentage of misdirected friendly shells fell in amongst us, as well as a few which were definitely hostile. We eagerly awaited the sound of the 25-pdrs. starting up, which would be the signal to go forward. At last the creeping barrage began, and the mighty armoured steam-roller started on its task to flatten out all before it.

At first we saw little sign of the enemy, and the few Germans we did see appeared completely dazed as they came in and gave themselves up. A German armoured car appeared from some woods on our right and made a dash for it right through the middle of us, unfortunately getting away with it, as the only tanks which could fire with any degree of safety were those in front and on either flank.

All went very much according to plan for the first five miles till we got to Grentheville. Here a "Moaning Minnie" opened up just in front of us, but before the last of its six barrels had been emptied the turrets of a dozen Shermans swung round and blew it and the crew to pieces—the best thing we had ever seen happen to this diabolical weapon.

It was at this time that the armoured groups were to emerge from the alley and fan out to their objectives. On we went to the outskirts of Hubert Folie, and found ourselves stuck out in front with no one upon either flank, and we were ordered to wait here until the opposition encountered on our left had been cleared up.

Shelling became rather unpleasant owing to our being in full observation of the enemy, and there was very little we could do about it. It was no use moving because the shells just kept on following us around.

In the meantime we were ordered to find out whether Hubert Folie was held. The approaches were all very open, so after a study of the air photographs of the village I decided to work a carrier section as close to the village as possible and then make a dash for it down the main street and out the other end. Diversionary fire was put down by the tanks and the carriers set off. After a few minutes of anxious waiting, they emerged from the village. David Stileman, who commanded the party, reported seeing no enemy, but as it turned out the next day, the village was in fact occupied. The enemy were presumably rather shaken by the sight of three carriers with all weapons blazing hurtling towards them at top speed, or else they did not wish to disclose their dispositions.

The Germans had by now obviously collected their wits together, after the first colossal onslaught, and things rapidly became very unpleasant for us. Armour-piercing shells began coming in from all directions and we were unable for a time to pinpoint where any of them were coming from and tanks of the 3rd R.T.R. began "brewing up." Then on our left, Panthers appeared and the fun really began. The tanks had pulled back to positions from where they could engage the enemy a little more safely, and I found that my half-track and a section of carriers were stuck out in front of them all. The best we could do was to move back to a hedge behind which we could at least get a little cover from view, although none from fire. Unfortunately, the carrier section suffered heavy casualties, and it was only a very small percentage of their strength which managed to join us at the hedge. Sergt. Fruin had done some wonderful work in getting them back, and his cool courage during this very unpleasant time was an example and inspiration to all around him.

We seemed to lie behind that hedge for hours, imagining every moment to be our last. I made a great mistake in passing round a bottle of gin, the effect of which lowered everyone's spirits instead of, as I had hoped, bolstering them up. During this period the Northants Yeomanry whom we had been awaiting, arrived, but they did not appear to be quite in the picture, and it was not long before they too were suffering disastrous losses.

Eventually we were able to pull back and rejoin the rest of the Company, who by this time were hard at work with their digging materials. Two German gunner observation posts with a wireless set had been discovered lying up just near them, and on their capture, the shelling died down considerably. Plans were then made for our night dispositions, and as a result we moved back behind a railway embankment, which must have saved many of our lives, as shortly after we had got into our new positions 88's opened up from the village of Bras and tanks began brewing up one after another. A very persistent "Moaning Minnie" was also sending over its missiles, which were dropping too close to be pleasant. So after our great start, we had ended up the day a very depleted force, and it was clear that we would be unable to carry out our original intention.

During the night, David Stileman took out a patrol to try and cut the Caen—Falaise road, but was unable to reach the objective owing to the many blazing tanks flood-lighting the countryside he had to cross.

So ended a day of thrills and disappointments. As a company, however, our losses might have been a great deal higher than they were, and we had netted in a good haul of prisoners. When light came next morning, we did not know what the day would have in store for us. A small comfort was that it surely could not be worse than the previous one. Our first move was to a big open field near the railway embankment, and we were accompanied by the 3rd R.T.R.'s remaining seventeen tanks. Here we were lucky, as the rest of this field, which was packed with vehicles, came in for some very heavy shelling, our part being left fairly well alone.

After lunch, orders came through that the remnants of the 29th Armoured Brigade were to capture Bras and Hubert Folie. "F" and "H" Companies were allotted Bras as their task, and we were to go through them and take on Hubert Folie.

Bras was successfully cleared and we went on to begin our attack on Hubert Folie. A very effective smoke-screen was put down by our 2-inch mortars and behind this 10 and 11 Platoons formed up and went in to the attack, followed by 12 Platoon, who were to consolidate in the rear. The village had been previously shelled and the tanks were pumping stuff into it too. As the motor platoons moved in I called over the air for the tanks to stop firing, but one went on firing and nothing could be done to stop it. It later transpired that this was a tank knocked out the day before and a German was manning its machine-gun. The carriers who were acting as flank protection ahead of the motor platoons came under fire from this machine-gun, and Cpl. Isard, a very old and popular member of the Company, was killed. We later had the satisfaction of seeing this German "brewed up" in no uncertain manner at very close range.

Meanwhile the clearing of the village was going well, and we were soon able to announce that it was in our hands completely and that we had collected a fair haul of prisoners as well as killing other enemy.

During this operation, my command vehicle was standing on the village green and, thinking that morale amongst my crew had not yet quite recovered from the previous day, I told my rear gunner, L./Cpl. Hodgson, that I had seen movement in a clump of bushes close at hand. Whereupon his Sten gun blazed into action and aggression became the keynote again. I have never dared to tell him that it was a put-up job, and I hope if he reads this he will not feel badly about it. At any rate, it produced exactly the effect which I had hoped it would.

We had had a lucky escape when thirty Focke-Wulf 190's appeared overhead, but they evidently had no clue as to what was going on and made off, dropping their long-range petrol tanks amongst us, and our gas experts rushed for their respirators.

It was not long before a battalion of our infantry brigade arrived on the scene and took over from us, enabling us to return once again to the railway embankment, where we rejoined the rest of the battalion in laager. Great confusion occurred on the way back for various reasons, but, as always mercifully seemed to happen, everyone turned up at the right place in the end. It had been a great day, and Hubert Folie was to head the list of villages and towns which fell into the Company's hands during the ensuing months.

It was now evident that the Bull had shot his bolt for the time being and that we would have to pull out to reorganize and refit. So accordingly next morning we moved back to the area of Demouville. Here it was very wet and muddy and once again we were in the middle of a gun area. However, in spite of these things, we spent a couple of quiet days here, the only enemy activity being a very occasional shell and the odd plane, and some much needed sleep and rest was enjoyed by all.

On the 22nd of July back we went, crossing the Orne once again by "London Bridge," and ending up at Cussy, in the neighbourhood of Caen, where we were really to have the chance again of getting ready for the next party. It was quite clear that the crust of German resistance round the bridgehead was very thick and was not easily to be cracked.

Coinciding with our arrival here, a long column of motor-cycles, jeeps and staff cars was seen approaching, and sitting in an open car together were Montgomery and Churchill. Many of us would have liked then to have peered into their minds and seen what they had in store for us in the future.

Our week at Cussy was very pleasant and nothing sensational happened. Much work was done and at the same time much rest and relaxation were also able to be included. Liberty trucks were run to Bayeux and we were given our first vacancies at rest camps, which were greatly enjoyed by those fortunate enough to go there. A notable event was the appearance of a N.A.A.F.I. mobile van, the first we had seen since leaving England and its contents were very quickly sold out.

A Spitfire made a forced landing in our lines one evening, but was promptly claimed to be in "E" Company's territory, a claim we did not dispute as we foresaw that someone would have to guard it. Kenneth Chabot was promoted to Captain, more reinforcements arrived, tank replacements appeared, and once again we were all set for the fray and in high spirits.

CHAPTER V

THROUGH THE BOCAGE

WE were now to try our luck alongside the Americans in the Caumont sector, which was the only part of the front where we had not yet battled, and it was during this operation that a captured German officer enquired whether the Bull was the Second Army sign.

On the 29th of July refreshed by our rest at Cussy we moved across the front to Bayeux and then turned south towards Caumont, ending up in some pleasant orchards a few miles north of the town.

Here we listened to a lecture by Norman Bourne, late of the 24th Lancers, on fighting in the Bocage, which dispelled any hopes we might have had of an easy passage to come. Right from the very beginning the word Bocage seemed to signify nothing but evil. Snipers thrived in it and could lie up for days quite safely, and the sniper complex at this time was at its height. In point of fact, they were nothing like as numerous as everyone liked to imagine and at times much too much caution was displayed on their behalf.

German aircraft were fairly active over the area and the next morning before light came 11 Platoon were bombed in their field. The cause was the lighting of a petrol fire in an adjoining field by another unit, and as was always the case, the punishment descended on the innocent. The bombs, however, all landed right in the centre of the field and the Platoon suffered no casualties.

A Holy Communion service was held before breakfast in this very peaceful setting amidst the fruit trees. The orchards of Normandy will probably remain for ever in our memories as cool, restful places in which our most peaceful hours were spent. There were obviously orchards which were an exception to this rule, but they were not many. Church services in settings such as this were always well attended, and during these difficult times religion undoubtedly played a bigger part in our lives than it had ever done before.

The morning was overcast and cloudy, but despite it the Royal Air Force delivered the goods, and at first light the 15th Scottish Division, with Churchill tanks of the Guards Brigade, attacked south of Caumont, and later in the day the 11th Armoured Division moved forward and passed through them at the village of Sept Vents. Shortly afterwards the Company took the lead and, pushing south, arrived before a small village just as dusk was falling. Enemy had been observed in the village and we were ordered to clear it as quickly as possible. The gunners, having laid on plans for an impressive "Stonk" on the place, informed me just before the attack was due to begin that they could not get permission to fire as higher formation did not think there were any enemy there; and, having no time to argue as darkness was fast coming on, I made a hasty arrangement with the troop leader of the 23rd Hussars to pump some shells into the village and the attack went in as previously planned, being carried out by 10 and 11 Platoons. In the village we found enemy equipment which had obviously been very recently abandoned, and one wounded German. However, it was very dark by now and it was useless trying to search the houses, so we spent the night very much on the alert and wondering what the morning would bring forth.

"H" Company had passed through us during the night, and in the morning, having searched our village and found nothing, we pushed on toward St. Martin des Besaces, where "H" Company were in trouble and had been pinned down. We were ordered to attack, supported by a squadron of the 3rd R.T.R. being given the information that the enemy consisted only of the odd sniper, and the three motor platoons accordingly went into the attack, the carriers being held in reserve. A high railway embankment had to be crossed and this obstacle could not be surmounted by the tanks and so they were unable to support the motor platoons. 10 and 11 Platoons came under heavy fire and were pinned down, suffering heavy casualties, but 12 Platoon managed to work round and reached their objective, although they lost a complete section on the way through mortaring. For several hours this handful of men of 12 Platoon held out on their objective against heavy odds, and Eric Yetman, who, although wounded, refused to go back, was awarded the Military Cross for this action. Eventually, with the aid of a battalion of the 15th Scottish Division and the 159th Brigade, the town was taken. St. Martin des Besaces had proved to be a much tougher nut to crack than higher command imagined, and the whole operation lacked co-ordination.

We had lost six killed in the action and a fair number wounded, including David Stileman and Eric Yetman, who were both evacuated. As a result, 11 Platoon had to be disbanded and split amongst 10 and 12 Platoons.

After a very short time for reorganization, we moved on through the Foret l'Evêque to La Ferrière, where the civilians gave us an enthusiastic welcome, and no enemy opposition was encountered on the way.

In the forest we ran parallel with the Americans, the unusual spectacle being witnessed of the Riflemen plying the marching Yanks with army biscuits, for which they appeared most grateful.

We spent the night with a squadron of the 3rd R.T.R., all being peaceful till stand-to next morning, when our area was sprayed by machine-gun fire coming, we later discovered, from an enemy tank which seemed to be rather out of the picture and which withdrew hurriedly when it realized what it was up against. The advance continued through some very lovely country to Beny Bocage, which we occupied after "F" Company had pushed north from the town.

Here we got our first real welcome of any size from the French people, and wine flowed freely, the local populace deciding unanimously that every available source of largess would be tapped.

Some idea of this rejoicing can be best illustrated by an account which Kingsmill sent home and which expressed in words many of our thoughts at the time :—

"We had a really wonderful experience this morning. If I may use the word, we helped to 'liberate' a fairish sized town. I have truly never before seen people go so absolutely mad with joy. Everybody was either shouting, waving, cheering, clapping, kissing one another, singing the 'Marseillaise' or doing all the whole lot at once. I wonder if I can give you the picture.

"The town square—market-place, I suppose, a fairish sized rectangle about eighty yards by twenty. At one end a Jerry tank, charred and blackened, still pours forth smoke. At the other end, where I am, there is a party going on in a hotel, you can see them from the open (very open—no glass) windows. Any soldier who can be 'spared' for a moment gets raked in.

"I, with headphones round neck, must perforce stay in my truck, but the back is 'open' and I can stand up and view the scene. A man comes up, smiling from ear to ear, and gives me a glass of champagne. A lovely drink it was, cool and bubbly; but before I know it my hand is seized by an old lady—about eighty-five, I should think—who shakes it madly and cries, 'Merci m'sieur—merci beaucoup.' She is nearly weeping for joy. It kind of gives you a lump in the throat to witness it. A gendarme is running up and down the square waving a huge tricolour, and more tricolours are flying everywhere—from telegraph poles (how the hell did they get there ?), one stuck in the fountain; most everybody has one somewhere in or around his house. Fresh 'Cross of Lorraine' armbands appear on young men who by their look are proud to be Frenchmen again, and not just lackeys. Another glass of wine is offered (and accepted), and more follows that. Flowers are thrown at you—nearly every truck has flowers on it. Then it's our turn; we give the people sweets. Some bars of chocolate and some cigarettes—no charity, it's a real pleasure to give them (they were rationed with two packets of 'Ersatz' cigarettes a month). Everybody is smoking—old men inhale, boys of two puff at them. Even a small girl is trying ! A little girl about five is skipping about like a lamb in springtime, accompanied by the crushing of already shattered glass as she jumps about. People are rushing here and there, to and fro—they're still kissing each other—mother and child, husband and wife, soldier and girl. Elation ? Ecstasy ? It's difficult to find a word that aptly describes it. It's a tremendous sight—and no one who witnessed it could ever forget. A Frenchman tells us he'd saved a machine-gun since the fall of France, and kept it in his house. This morning, the day he had been waiting for, he got nine Jerries with it.

"The little girl is back again, with her brown eyes and curly hair—keeps wanting to shake my hand. So does everybody else, it seems. The whole town's gone crazy—crazy with joy. It's wonderful."

After a brief period of rejoicing we moved forward again with a squadron of the 3rd R.T.R. and reached St. Charles de Percy, thus cutting the main highway from Caen to Vire. The houses on the crossroads were cleared without much difficulty, and prisoners were taken, in addition to a collection of enemy soft vehicles which were successfully brewed by the tanks.

It was evident that we had cut one of the enemy's main escape routes from the north, and we anxiously waited to see what would be his reaction to our move. We settled down astride the crossroads and it was not long before an enemy tank approached from the north and we could see movement of enemy armour to the south. Our chances of holding off an armoured attack in any strength were not bright with the forces we had at our disposal, so after urgent appeals for help over the air, some self-propelled 17-pdrs. were put under our command and we were further strengthened by the loan of a motor platoon from "H" Company. The expected counter-attack never came, but the threat of it kept us all very keyed up for the rest of the day and night, our only aggressive action, however, being taken by the mortars in the form of a very good shoot on enemy movement on the Vire road to our south.

We laid Hawkins grenades freely across the roads leading to our positions, and the next day began with an unfortunate incident when an armoured car of the Inns of Court Regiment was blown up on a grenade we had failed to pick up. Not a great deal of damage, however, was done to the car, and the occupants, though slightly shaken, were not seriously injured.

The enemy, during the night had, except for a few armoured cars, withdrawn from the area immediately in front of us, and it was not long before we moved on again still southwards through the village of Beaulieu towards Presles. Nothing much happened till, just short of Presles, we engaged a patrol of Panzer Grenadiers and took a prisoner, one of the most enormous blond Aryans I have ever seen. The remainder of the patrol unfortunately got away, although it must have been severely shaken by the hail of mortar bombs which fell round it. As evening drew on, we passed through Presles and the whole Battalion, with the 23rd Hussars, took up a position on some high ground at Bas Perier. This high ground was extremely vital to the Germans and we confidently expected to be heavily counter-attacked at first light next morning. Digging up here was very difficult, but our perseverance paid ample dividends, as will be seen by the events of the ensuing days.

The expected dawn counter-attack, to our surprise, did not materialize, but it was not long however, before we realized that we were in for a warm day. German infantry could be seen streaming back into Presles, thus cutting our centre line, and shortly after this, tanks and self-propelled guns, most concealed in sunken roads, opened up from all sides. "Moaning Minnies" added to the fun and soon tanks began "brewing up" and casualties began to mount. Morale dropped and I think came nearer to cracking than at any other time during our whole campaign in Europe. In my own humble opinion, the sole saving grace was the quite magnificent work done by Michael Wilcox and the Medical Officer of the 23rd Hussars with their stretcher-bearers. Despite the very many calls on them, at no time were wounded or dead left unattended for more than a few seconds. No praise can be too high for their work, all of which had to be done under heavy fire ; and owing to the cut centre line, no casualties could be evacuated, which meant a greatly added strain on their resources.

Amongst our own casualties in the Company, John Priestley was very badly wounded and died the next day. His coolness and bravery had inspired his platoon, and his death was a very great loss to us both as a leader and a friend.

Vehicles, too, had come in for a bad time and we had four half-tracks and a carrier hit. One spark of humour which I shall never forget, however, was the sight of our inimitable "Ack-Ack" Jones, standing up in a slit trench, his face wreathed in smiles, regarding the winch on his half-track hanging on by the merest thread. Such things as this happily stand out in my memory more than all the other unpleasant sights, which were all too common at this time.

During the day we had sent out two patrols to Chenedolle, a few miles to the south of us. The first of these, led by Sergt. Kisby, was in the form of a reconnaissance and the village was reported clear of enemy. The second, led by Cpl. Griggs, consisted of a "P.I.A.T. gang," which lay up in the village, waiting for enemy tanks which, however, did not put in an appearance.

Night descended and we settled down, knowing that no supplies could reach us and that none of our wounded could be sent back. Many volunteers could have been found to pilot an ambulance column back, but owing to sniping on the previous day of our stretcher-bearers and ambulances, it was considered best not to make the attempt. We were, however, relieved to hear that a battalion of the Warwicks had been rushed up to attack Presles, and to clear our centre line. After a tremendous barrage, they accomplished this task with little difficulty, and at first light a patrol from "H" Company, established contact with them, thus ending our period of being cut off from the outside world, and so enabling an ambulance column to be formed immediately and our casualties to be evacuated.

The 4th of August was another day of being shelled and "minnied" and again a "P.I.A.T. gang" went to Chenedolle. It was, however, much more comforting than the previous day inasmuch as we knew that at least we could not be fired on from our immediate rear. Our padre, Jeff Taylor, who had been up with us the whole time, held a simple impressive burial service for those killed on the previous day, during which service perhaps by mere coincidence, not a shot was fired by either side.

The next day we heard with relief that the Warwicks were moving up to take over our position and that we were withdrawing to Presles. Their reconnaissance parties arrived up in the morning and were heralded by the arrival of some misguided Typhoons who, having fired one rocket into our area, were dissuaded from further aggressive action by dense clouds of yellow smoke—our recognition signal for friendly aircraft.

Prior to the arrival of the main body of the Warwicks, Sergt. McEwen, who had previously taken out a patrol to lie up in observation of Chenedolle, returned with the news that enemy infantry and tanks were moving up. Shortly afterwards a counter-attack developed, which was broken up by artillery fire, and it was actually during this counter-attack that we effected the change over with the Warwicks, moving back on foot to Presles, where we took up a position in the orchards on the slopes above the village. The vehicles could not be moved till dark and the Company Sergeant-Major was left in charge of them. When they did eventually rejoin us, except for a few essential ones, they were all concentrated about a mile behind us to minimize the loss by shelling.

For five more days Presles was to be our home, a period spent for the most part in or extremely near slit trenches and clad in our steel helmets. These precautions were very well worth while, and considering the intensity of shelling and mortaring our total of a dozen casualties was not unduly high. Brian Oxley-Boyle returned and took over 12 Platoon, but two days after his arrival he went on patrol, from which he never came back. He had gone forward on his own, wearing a 38 wireless set and many other accoutrements of war, when he was pounced on and carried unceremoniously away. We were later relieved to hear he was a prisoner and that months later he had been liberated when the Americans overran his prison camp at Brunswick. Peter Morley was wounded very early on, and thereafter 9, 10 and 12 Platoons were commanded by Sergts. Kisby, Carr and Macaulay respectively. No one could ever wish to have three more loyal, conscientious and inspiring platoon commanders than these three sergeants, who had the complete confidence of the men under their command.

We were never actually attacked here, but several times we brought our supporting artillery down on suspected infiltration. Patrols were sent out with varying degrees of success, and everyone became compass conscious, taking bearings on every sound of an enemy gun or mortar. We were encouraged in this latter practice by hearing that it had helped our gunners in their multiple tasks.

The nights on the whole were quieter than the day, and there was most mornings a very welcome early morning mist which, while it lasted, enabled us to move about quite freely. One night, however, the "Minnies" came down in no uncertain manner, causing havoc in the orchards and setting hedges and trees on fire, as well as a house in 10 Platoon's area full of teller mines and explosives.

Communications were very difficult and it was a veritable nightmare for signallers. Lines and wireless leads were being continually broken by shell fire, and the signallers did a great job of work counteracting these difficulties.

Two items of humour stand out. The first when Sergt. Crisp and Cpl. Carter arrived up one day, in a jeep, and stopped on the corner outside Company H.Q. Some unkind members of the Company informed them that the enemy undoubtedly had the jeep on fixed lines and were merely waiting till they returned to it before it was blown to smithereens. By dint of crawling, the two prominent members of the Motor Transport Club eventually leapt into the vehicle and an enormous cloud of dust, was the signal to the German gunners that they had missed shooting up a valuable target. The second incident was intensely humorous on reflection, but at the time was really very alarming. A platoon of Vickers machine-guns had moved into the battalion area just above the Company entirely unbeknown to us, its role being to support the Warwicks on Bas Perier. One night when all those not on duty were well away in the land of dreams, this platoon opened up and our minds were not turning over quickly enough at that hour to recognize them as Vickers machine-guns. I, for one, thought we were at least surrounded and began crawling on my stomach to the command trench where Kenneth Chabot was on the air. On my way I noticed other members of Company H.Q. performing the same movements as myself, and I later heard from unreliable sources that one Rifleman had woken up and jumped straight out of his slit trench with his hands clasped on the back of his head.

Twice we were going to be relieved from this unhealthy position and twice for various operational reasons we were disappointed at the last moment. Eventually on the night of 10th of August the magic code word "Swallow" came over the air, and with a sigh of relief we streamed out of our positions back to our transport, which carried us back to the Beny Bocage area again, where the Echelon had a most welcome hot meal awaiting us, and where we needed no encouragement to lie down and sleep.

CHAPTER VI

ON TO LAIGLE

In the setting of two very pleasant cornfields and a clover field we quickly took stock, and a windfall in the shape of a complete motor company of the 8th Battalion King's Royal Rifle Corps arrived to swell the Battalion's very depleted numbers. Enough men arrived to reform 11 Platoon and all we had to do was to find four new platoon commanders. These were produced from widespread sources. James Ramsden brought his headquarters and a complete carrier section and assumed command of 9 Platoon. Donald Sudlow came to us from "H" Company, Dick May from Retford, and Michael Anderson from "F" Company, and these three took over 10, 11 and 12 Platoons respectively.

Only two days to sort ourselves out were allowed, and on the 13th of August we set off once more to take over from a battalion of the Seaforths of the 15th Scottish Division who were holding a position at Drury to the west of Beny Bocage.

We moved in after dark, leaving most of our transport some way behind, and all seemed quite peaceful save for the odd rifle shot fired at random in our direction. What few vehicles we did try and take with us got hopelessly stuck in a sunken lane together with some transport of "F" Company. Both parties were under the second sunrays and that great combination of Kenneth Chabot and Ricky Greville tried for hours in vain to get on the move again, their feelings being somewhat embittered by the Colonel who, arriving on the scene in the morning, told them to do something about it.

Rumours were flying round at this time of a great German withdrawal, and the remarkable progress of the Americans to the south was already threatening to encircle completely the German Seventh Army. These rumours, as turned out afterwards, had a good deal of foundation, but we still had fresh in our minds the memories of the earlier battles, where each time we were told the enemy was pulling out, a violent counter-attack developed, and we resolved to decide for ourselves when the withdrawal could be publicly announced.

Nothing very unpleasant troubled us during our stay here and we were all quite rested when on the 15th of August we began our partnership with "A" Squadron of the 23rd Hussars, commanded by David Turquand, an old friend of ours from the 24th Lancers.

After a quiet morning on the road leading south to Vassy, we passed through the leading group, and it was not long before the first tank was "brewed up" outside the village of Canteloup, referred to over the radio as "the fruity village," which was found to be held by the enemy.

An attack, supported by the tanks, was launched and 11 Platoon on the right pushed into the village without meeting serious opposition; 10 Platoon, however, on the left were held up and suffered casualties, three of them being fatal. With darkness coming on, it was decided to withdraw the motor platoons, leaving 9 Platoon to consolidate on the cross-roads on the outskirts, while the remainder of us went firm farther back.

An amusing incident occurred at Company H.Q. during the attack, when a German appearing out of the hedge, and wanting to surrender, tapped Bishop on the shoulder, the latter being so taken aback that he nearly gave himself up to the German instead, and even his inevitable pipe was said to have fallen to the ground.

After an unpleasant night of shelling and mortaring, during which our anti-tank platoon from "E" Company suffered casualties, the advance in the morning continued without any serious opposition to the high ground north of Vassy, where we were sharply shelled on arrival. This subsided, however, and we settled down here for the night after James Ramsden and Sergt. Kisby had gone out on a reconnaisance and had been chased back by a Tiger tank, one round taking the skin off James's nose.

Our first comparative "swan" began the following day and continued for some hours as we passed through St. Germain and Athis to the banks of the River Rouore. Here "H" Company found the bridge to be blown, but by dint of brushwood and other forms of home-made bridging material made the river fordable and formed a bridgehead on the far bank. Through this we passed and the village of Notre Dame de Rocher was attacked by 10 and 12 Platoons, supported by "A" Squadron, 23rd Hussars. The enemy withdrew, but 10 Platoon were mortared on their objective and 9 Platoon had suffered some casualties from sniping, after successfully occupying some farm buildings which overlooked the village. Eventually 10 and 12 Platoons came out of the village and 11 Platoon, with the leading troop of tanks and section of carriers, continued the advance. They very soon ran into trouble and, as always seemed to happen, at this juncture we had to call it off owing to failing light. Our night position was mortared and shelled continuously and more casualties were caused.

One of the lighter highlights of the day, however, was the report of Kenneth Chabot over the rear link of the information that we had opposing us the "Notre Dame de Rocher Regiment" This legendary formation caused many heartburns on the part of the Intelligence staff. The originator was quite convinced of the validity of the report and to this day resents the fun poked at him on the subject by the less serious-minded members of the Battalion.

We were now beginning to get used to the German habit of fighting a rearguard action till nightfall and then pulling out, and the following day was no exception to this rule. "B" Squadron and "F" Company went through and "swanned" merrily on, meeting no opposition, and we reached the high ground overlooking Putanges, on our old friend the River Orne. Some pleasant parkland served as a harbour for us for the day, while we awaited the making of a bridgehead and the building of a bridge.

At last light a force under my command, consisting of 11 and 12 Platoons, a machine-gun platoon from "E" Company and a troop of self-propelled 17-pdrs., took up a position overlooking the proposed bridgehead, the object being to deal with any enemy who might try and counter-attack in the morning. The remainder of the Company remained where it was under Kenneth Chabot. No counter-attack developed, however, but the machine-gunners found an excuse to open up and, as was always the case, once they had begun there was nothing in the world which would persuade them to stop.

Eventually the two portions of the Company joined up again and on we went east till we came to the village of Cui. Here the leading tank was knocked out and thereafter a strange and uneasy situation developed. The village contained a large hospital which was full of German wounded, and which seemed to have an enormous medical staff, many of whom I am quite sure acquired red-cross armbands a very short time before we arrived on the scene. There were large numbers of seriously wounded Germans and some German nurses, who when not on duty appeared to be practising their feminine charms most effectively and blatantly on the walking wounded cases.

We remained trying to clear up this situation for the rest of the day, and as darkness came on a party under James Ramsden set out to stalk a Tiger tank we had seen clearly behind a hedge. Up went the parachute flares and the P.I.A.Ts. prepared to fire from what we hoped was almost point-blank range, but the Tiger had slipped away just previously in the general noise and confusion.

Orders then came through to pull back from the village for the night and we retired to an area where we found a perfectly good abandoned Panther. Here we "dossed down" for the few remaining hours of the night still left to us.

The position at Cui next morning was exactly the same as when we had left it the night before with the exception that this time we were not greeted by any hostile fire. After crossing the Falaise-Argentan highway at Occagnes, we approached the Foret de Gouffern with a certain amount of caution, as several clearly camouflaged objects could be seen in the edge of the wood. Under cover of smoke, and after we had brought down a few precautionary rounds of gunfire on the wood itself, a patrol went forward and fired a P.I.A.T. bomb at one of these objects. A direct hit was scored, but on clear examination the object turned out to be an abandoned German tank and the other objects we had seen in addition also turned out to be the same. Accordingly a section of carriers moved forward, but the leading one went up on a mine and once again the advance was slowed down. The woods either side of the road obviously had to be cleared by the motor platoons on foot and this plan was set in motion. More traces of mines were found and booby-trapped trees had been pulled across the road, but with the aid of our sappers these were cleared and the vehicles began moving forward again.

It was at this stage that 12 Platoon, moving forward on foot, captured General Kurt Badinsky, commanding 271 Infantry Division, and his entire staff. An old lady had rushed up to them and told them that there were some Germans in a certain farmhouse, whereupon, on closer investigation, a General was seen at the window and was immediately covered while the remainder of the Platoon surrounded the buildings. Staff officers, clerks, and orderlies came tumbling out and very soon the complete Divisional Headquarters personnel were assembled in the courtyard, being enthusiastically searched. The old general, who had no idea what was happening around him, and who had no division left to command, was particularly anxious to surrender to an officer and refused to believe Michael Anderson was one, and when I arrived on the scene I had considerable difficulty in making him believe that I was not a non-commissioned officer. He found it very hard to believe that dress of British officers in action was almost identical to that of their men, and when the Colonel arrived, looking equally dusty and shabby, he was never more exasperated. A request was granted to him to say goodbye to his staff and, after much heel-clicking and saluting, the first live German General we had ever seen was driven away to captivity, leaving behind him two very fine cars, which were very quickly snapped up.

This advance had brought us on to the edge of the famous Falaise pocket at Bailleul and here we took up our position for the night, seeing for ourselves some of the fantastic destruction of German war material. The ceaseless pounding by our guns and aircraft of the remnants of the German Seventh Army in the pocket continued all the time, and for once that sort of sound was rhythm to our ears.

Morale was high and soared even higher when plans for the next day were announced. A peace-time march along good roads appeared the form and in this we were not to be disappointed. After passing through the battered town of Argentan we overtook the Echelon, which had raced to the fore, then on through Exmes to the neighbourhood of Gacé, which we reached at nightfall.

Opposition was again conspicuous by its absence the following day, except for mines which had been laid at nearly every crossroads we came to, and booby-trapped trees across the road. James Ramsden and the carriers, however, found an excellent way round and we arrived much quicker than we had dared to hope on the broad highway to Laigle, up which we streamed in no uncertain manner, getting an enthusiastic welcome from the civilians all along the way.

It was decided to halt the column above the town and James, with a section of carriers double banking some American jeeps which had swanned in from another direction, entered Laigle on the 22nd of August, a date which marked a milestone in our long march of liberation. Their reception was terrific, and after doing a victorious tour of the town they rejoined us as we moved into a pleasant field which we learnt was to be our home for the next few days.

CHAPTER VII

THE GREAT "SWAN"

IN a very short time Laigle became a back area and the roads were jammed with transport of the 43rd and 50th Divisions, racing forward to the Seine.

While these preparations were being made for the infantry assault across the Seine, we settled down to enjoy about a week of relaxation in the lovely summer weather we were now having. In our area was a very attractive mill-pond and this served to good advantage as our private swimming-pool. In addition to E.N.S.A. and cinema shows, everyone was allowed to walk out round the neighbouring countryside, and there was even a dance laid on in Laigle, to which, unfortunately, very few of the gentle sex came, it being reported from authoritative sources that the only member of the Company who had a dance was our local Romeo, Sergt. Hadley. And, last but not least, much valuable work was done in the form of reorganisation and preparation for our next party. Reinforcements arrived, and Mickey McCrea returned to the Company just before the time once more came to think in terms of orders of battle and centre lines.

The 43rd Division's bridgehead at Vernon being established, we said farewell to Laigle early on the morning of the 28th of August, having previously teamed up again with our "sandy" friends, the 3rd Royal Tank Regiment. Our route lay along very dry and dusty roads through Evreux and we harboured just short of Vernon, where we had time for a very welcome meal and brew.

Nothing much was known of our future. All we knew was that we were going to cross the Seine and push on presumably in a north-easterly direction. The strength of the opposition we were going to meet was impossible to gauge, but the general opinion was that it was likely to be a degree stiffer than that described in the previous chapter.

This estimate was not lowered when, immediately after crossing the Seine at Vernon, we came upon a knocked-out Tiger tank, still smouldering, and lying on it several charred bodies. Nightfall found us in some fields on the high ground just across the river, with the sound of battle very close ahead.

Opposition for the first part of the next day was very slight and, having cleared several small villages on the way, Etrepagny was reached without much difficulty; and here we received a most enthusiastic welcome from the civilians, who, however, suffered a bitter disappointment when, shortly after we had left, the Germans came back and all rejoicing had to subside at once. However, it was not long before the situation was restored again.

The tanks had a small battle near Mainneville and, having disposed of the opposition, we arrived a short distance south of Amecourt, where we settled down for the night.

Kenneth Chabot, who had been taking things easy in "A.1" Echelon for the day, on rejoining us for the night was, to his great surprise and horror, ordered to take a patrol out to see whether Amecourt was held. The patrol consisted of 12 Platoon, and a section of carriers, and Kenneth, having recovered from the first shock, and having steadied himself with a large swig from the whisky bottle, sallied forth into the night with his party. The description of that patrol can best be told in his own words, which I now quote.

"I set forth with my party on a compass bearing, travelling on the leading carrier, but had some doubts as to where we should eventually arrive owing to the large amount of metal around being liable to render the compass inaccurate. However, I had more or less memorised the route before we started and knew that we had to leave a farm on our left. I was therefore very relieved when the farm loomed up in the darkness, but beyond it also appeared a number of objects which looked like vehicles. Our fears were set at rest, however, when on closer investigation these turned out to be bushes. We then went forward again and soon reached the point where we had decided to get out of our vehicles. My orders were to find out if there were any enemy in the village and also to ascertain if the road through the village was suitable for tanks. On the map there was a track marked running straight down to the bridge, and I also had to find out if this was negotiable for vehicles. I accordingly sent off a party from the carriers to go through the village and took with me two sections of 12 Platoon with a view to "recceing" the track, and afterwards working up towards the village. The remaining section I left to look after the vehicles. I can say here and now that we never found the track that night, although we spent some four hours looking for it, wandering through the fields of lucerne, knee-deep and soaking wet, and down precipices through the woods. In the darkness it was quite impossible to move quietly and I decided it was definitely "not on" to approach the bridge through the woods. I therefore told Goldsmith to report this back on his 38 wireless set. He set about this task, speaking at the top of his extremely penetrating voice, thereby multiplying greatly the number of grey hairs in my head. He failed to get through so we made one further attempt to locate this elusive track. Most of the men with me were freshly out from England, and I can only think that they had had very little, if any, night training, as moving along I had the sensation of having a herd of elephants following me. Looking back on it now, I am appalled at the risks we took that night. I had no more luck this time, so I took my party back to the vehicles, where I found that the party sent into the village had returned. Sergt. Nibbs told me that the road through the village was suitable for tanks and that the place was definitely held. I decided that I would like to know more about the enemy, so before light came I took with me two men into the village. We had not got very far before we heard someone coming along the road and we dived for the ditch. As this person approached, however, I saw it was a civilian, so I stopped him, but nearly had a heart attack when he started shouting and cheering on realising we were English. Having calmed him down, I learnt from him that there were approximately four hundred Germans in the village belonging to an artillery regiment. All were asleep, he said, except a few who were harnessing horses into carts. I heard this going on and as it was now getting light we made our way back to our vehicles and found that the rest of the Company had just arrived on the scene."

First light came and we went forward with the tanks to Amecourt. The operation to clear the village commenced, but did not get very far as opposition was much stiffer than we had imagined, and we withdrew to the outskirts again, where we took up a defensive position. In the meantime the command half-track had been knocked out by a 20 mm. gun and the crew, who baled out, sniped. Isham was killed and everyone else wounded, with the exception of Kingsmill, who remained on the wireless giving us information, displaying great coolness and courage, which won for him the Military Medal. And so for the second time Mickey McCrea began the long journey back to England, his luck being really out.

After we had shelled the village, it was decided to by-pass it, leaving the 159th Brigade to do the clearing, and to cross the River Epte at Serifontaine. In the meantime the patrol had rejoined us, bringing with it a useful haul of prisoners, and we set off with between fifty and sixty Germans on the bonnets of our half-tracks.

A mortar carrier was left behind, and shortly after we had left ninety-odd Germans came out of the village and surrendered to the crew of four men. A further fifty prisoners were handed over to them by the Squadron of the 3rd Royal Tank Regiment, which remained with them, and driving this great throng in front of them, they eventually succeeded in delivering them to a prisoner-of-war cage, catching up the company shortly afterwards.

This operation had taken a certain amount of time and the 23rd Hussars and "H" Company had gained the lead in what we now began to realize had the possibilities of being a far greater and speedier advance than we had ever dared to hope. We followed on behind until Marseille-en-Beauvais, where we passed through the 23rd Hussars group, to regain the lead once more.

The only opposition in our path came mainly from "swanning" Germans who had no clue as to what was happening and were therefore much too surprised at seeing our armoured column streaming down the road to worry us unduly. Crevecoeur-le-Grand was entered with little difficulty, the local inhabitants giving us the greatest welcome we had yet had.

The town's gendarmes were giving away numerous cases of brandy and the Company had its fair share. Here, too, we saw our first real evidence of the treatment of collaborators. Women's heads were shaved and many other indignities were suffered by these people, who no doubt deserved all they got. On the other hand, it was not a pleasant sight to see, and one could not help wondering how many private feuds were being settled under the cloak of collaboration.

After leaving Crevecoeur our way lay through a wooded valley, almost in the form of a ravine, with sides rising steeply. A certain amount of caution was necessary here, as a few well-sited anti-tank guns, supported by determined infantry, could have made things very unpleasant for us. But no opposition was met, and as darkness fell we entered Croissy-sur-Selle, where we halted to await further orders.

Company H.Q. commandeered a house for a meal, and the eggs were still sizzling in the frying pan when Colonel Silvertop, whose personal leadership inspired us all, received the order couched in the now famous phrase, "It's moonlight tonight." The parlour where we were cooking was the most suitable place to give out orders, and so, hastily eating what we could, the room was cleared for the order group, which assembled in this typical little French cottage kitchen, dimly lit by the light of lanterns. Only one question was asked, "What do we do when we get to Amiens?" and this was later answered by the Brigadier by the words "Knock at the door and see if they will let you in." A troop of tanks of the 3rd Royal Tank Regiment, was to lead, followed by "G" Company complete, with the remainder of the 3rd Royal Tank Regiment tailing on behind. The distance was approximately twenty miles and only one village lay on our route.

To this village James Ramsden and the Signal Officer of the 3rd Royal Tank Regiment were dispatched in advance to see if it was held and to collect any available information from the civilians living there.

When they reported all was clear, the advance began in pouring rain, making it exceedingly difficult for our expected ally, the moon, to play its prescribed part. It was altogether a strange and at times, frightening sensation to be ploughing on through enemy territory in the dark and having not the faintest idea of what might be in our path. Everyone was feeling very tired and I had to get the sergeant-major to ride up and down the column in a scout car to make sure the drivers of carriers in particular did not fall asleep at the wheel and cause a hold up of the column.

In general, enemy opposition on the way was either "brewed up" or run over. German vehicles joined the column from side roads and sometimes travelled several miles with us before we realised their presence. Coloured lights were always being reported ahead, and there is no doubt that many of us that night were quite convinced that we had seen various objects which in point of fact never existed. At one time a large dark object appeared in front of us and the leading tank fired a round at it. The most gigantic explosion occurred, and the object, which turned out to be an armoured ammunition carrier, disolved into small fragments. At the sound of the explosion a German was seen to spring up near my half-track and run faster than I have ever seen anyone run before. Gearing raced after him, but soon gave up the chase, and to this day we like to think that that German is still running and unable to stop himself. At any rate, we were able to relieve our somewhat frayed nerves at this time by a good laugh at this unfortunate Hun's expense.

Light came on the morning of the 31st of August, and we found ourselves on the threshold of Amiens. The first sign of enemy activity was some very surprised German soldiers on bicycles, who rode into our column and were promptly put in the bag. They had obviously had a night out in the town and were cycling back to their appointed stations in the neighbouring villages, and this appeared to them a poor end to their carousing activities.

Bill Close, commanding the leading Squadron of 3rd Royal Tank Regiment, and I were then given orders to enter Amiens, push through the centre of the city and seize the bridges over the Somme. Reports came in from civilians that there were approximately five thousand Germans in Amiens, and at that early hour and having had no sleep, this information shook us a bit. Still, orders were orders, and we decided to push straight on, keeping to the main streets and making no diversions in case we got split up into small parties. If we were bold and quick we reckoned we could probably get to our objective before the Germans realised we were in the city, because it was quite obvious that up to the present they had not the slightest inkling of the presence of a British armoured column within miles of them.

It was now getting really light and we could see enemy columns and single vehicles streaming into the city along roads running parallel to our own, and a certain amount of confused shooting took place. It was at this juncture that Harwin picked up a German bazooka and it went off in his hand, gliding between my half-track and the scout car and exploding against a road block in front of us. It is still an extremely debatable point as to who was most surprised by this untoward incident—Harwin, the occupants of my half-track, or the bazooka itself. The old adage "curiosity killed the cat" very nearly rang true that time.

After a certain amount of discussion, negotiation, and I might even add, argument as to who should go first, the leading section of carriers and the leading troop of tanks arrived at a compromise by which they advanced abreast.

To cut a long story short, we entered Amiens, the fighting inside the city developing into a series of individual platoon actions, in which all achieved notable success and the Germans forces were knocked clean off their balance and mopped-up before they really had any chance of realizing what was happening. The most famous of these little battles was enacted by 10 Platoon and was glamorously described by the press as "Sudlow's Shooting Gallery." I cannot do better than quote an extract from the columns of the many provincial papers in which this story was published :—

"What is described in the Battalion as 'Sudlow's Shooting Gallery' was one of the features of the fighting in Amiens, where the Nazis, taken completely by surprise, endeavoured to get out of the city quickly and safely. Lieut. Donald Sudlow saw that as few as possible did so.

"He was in command of the leading platoon of a battalion of the 11th Armoured Division, which entered Amiens side by side with the tanks. On the platoon's way down the main street it was noticed that a big Hitler barracks had received the attention of our bombers. A road ran alongside the barracks and at the far end connected up with another parallel main road into the city.

"The latter appeared to be popular with retreating Germans, so Lieut. Sudlow put out three Bren gun teams behind piles of rubble and covered the far end of the connecting road, much in the style of a rifle range.

"The first target was a lorry, which came tearing round the corner and was stopped dead with simultaneous bursts from the Brens. Then a section of infantry tried to double across the opening. Of the dozen who tried only two succeeded. Another lorry gasped to a standstill and some more infantry fared even worse, for by now the marksmen were getting warmed up and competition was pretty keen.

"A staff car almost made the crossing, but was stopped by a brilliant shot, which killed the driver. The passenger jumped out and dived for cover under one of the lorries. The lorry was shot up. A large number of infantry tried to silence the post but failed miserably. Fifty prisoners were taken and as many left wounded or dead. The scene at the far end of the road was indescribable."

These sort of incidents were taking place wherever our platoons moved and they were all in terrific form. After forcing our way right through the city, 11 Platoon were just about to put in an attack on a bridge when it was rudely blown before our eyes. However, the main bridge had been saved and still keeping pretty alert, we settled down for a much-needed wash and brush up. We had not long to wait before an S.S. car drove straight into us, skidded round with machine-guns blazing and unfortunately made a getaway. Breakfast tasted wonderful that morning and, despite our weariness, we felt on top of the world, but even then we found it hard to realize what an historic advance we had achieved. On tuning into the B.B.C. for the eight o'clock news we were amused to hear that we were still some thirty miles short of Amiens but going very well. The next thing to do was to check up and find out if everyone was present and to hope for the arrival of the Echelon. Our casualties had been very light, considering the amount of street fighting we had done.

The Echelon had been gallantly chasing us, having had to cover enormous distances to and from supply points, and often running into parties of enemy with whom we had not had time to deal. And as if nothing untoward had been happening, the supply lorries arrived and the work of replenishing our thirsty vehicles began. Rations and mail were also on board, the latter being always the most welcome of the many varied forms of service our "Q" staff undertook for us.

Sergt. Fruin's mortar carrier, which had dropped out of the column during the night ride, rejoined us at this stage of affairs and yet another fantastic story of the night's happenings was revealed, which Sergt. Fruin told me as follows :—

"We remained in the column till about 4 a.m., when without any warning the engine of the carrier spluttered and finally stopped. By the time we had verified the fact that we had run out of petrol, the column had left us behind, and we had not the faintest idea where we were. We stopped several vehicles which came along, but the answer was always the same, 'Sorry, chaps, nearly out ourselves,' so we decided the only thing to do was to wait for the Echelon, which we knew would be following on behind.

"By this time the sun was just coming up and we found ourselves on a stretch of road which was lined with trees. A good ditch on the left-hand side we decided would be an excellent place for a brew and a spot of breakfast, which was well under way when Cripps spotted the Echelon emerging from a wood on what appeared to be the road on which we had halted. The very misty dawn, however, had deceived us, and imagine our surprise when we discovered that the Echelon was a German one moving along a side road, joining our road about fifty yards behind us.

"The column was still about six hundred yards from us when we opened up with all our available weapons, consisting of one Bren gun and three rifles, in an effort to bring them to a halt as far away as possible. The column was clear of the wood and we could now see consisted of eleven three-ton lorries and a "Volkswagen." We managed to stop one of the vehicles in the middle of the column, but this had no effect on the others who were approaching the turning on to our road. We simply could not miss the leading vehicle and, letting the driver's cab have a burst, it came to a standstill amid clouds of steam, only thirty yards from us. Two Germans leapt out of the back and dived for the ditch, but that was the last thing they ever did.

"The remainder of the column panicked and drove off the road in all directions, to no avail, however, as within the next few seconds we had 'brewed up' four more vehicles and the others just stopped, their crews baling out. The next half-hour was spent in playing hide-and-seek in the corn, exchanging shot for shot, and we collected in twenty-three prisoners, counting in addition five dead and nine wounded. Our own casualties consisted of one spoilt brew.

"One of the prisoners spoke a little English, so we told him to go and get some petrol from his vehicles. This he seemed only too pleased to do and, having filled up, we continued our journey to rejoin the rest of the Company."

I have so far mentioned nothing of the reception we got from the inhabitants of Amiens. There was no doubt that they were just as surprised to see us as the Germans were, and it was therefore not till some time later that, the premature shock having worn off, they really expressed any emotion over their liberation. Signs of hardships and privations suffered by the townspeople were more evident here than in any other place we had previously entered, and this no doubt was largely the cause for the wave of looting, mainly of foodstuffs, which swept the town. An enormous food dump alongside which we came to rest was invaded by a vast crowd of people and the place emptied in a fantastically short time.

After a quick lunch we crossed the Somme and harboured in some woods on the high ground on the far bank. It was evident that the Germans had hoped to make a stand on the Somme, and on the far bank were numerous abandoned guns. We also found a dump of brand new guns in a cemetery on the outskirts of Amiens.

The woods where we now found ourselves had been used as a German artillery headquarters, which could only have been abandoned a very short time before our arrival. A field kitchen contained an excellent ready-cooked meal, which was unfortunately at the headquarters of the 3rd Royal Tank Regiment. This, however, did not stop Watts from shovelling other loot and brandy into my scout car while I was getting orders.

We were not going to move forward till the morning, so our replenishment having been completed, there was nothing left to do but settle down to the first night's proper sleep since leaving Laigle. Everyone was very tired indeed and no inducement was needed to curl up in our blankets, laid down on the pine needle carpet of this most pleasant resting-place.

We still did not know what lay ahead of us or what our destination was, but owing to the chaos and confusion reigning at this time in the German army we felt confident that our force, consisting of an armoured regiment and a motor company, was stronger than anything the Germans could produce.

Refreshed by our good night's rest, we set off next morning in very high spirits, and we pushed on steadily all day, meeting very little opposition and nothing spectacular occurring.

One very pleasing factor, however, was the great number of flying bomb sites, many still in the early stages of construction, we were finding abandoned. Nearly all of us were Londoners and it was very gratifying to know that we were helping very considerably to lessen the burdens and dangers of that great city and of our own homes.

The Maquis all along our route were in great form and had performed many brave deeds, on more than one occasion being of inestimable value to us. They were the solution to the prisoner problem and we used to carry our prisoners on our vehicles, handing them over to the first organized band of Maquis we met. We assisted the Maquis in their battles wherever possible, but there were occasions when we had to refuse aid to them, owing to the importance of moving on with the greatest possible speed, and they were undoubtedly sometimes disappointed that we had seemingly left them in the lurch. In the excitement of the moment, it must have appeared to these brave patriots that their little local battle in their own home town was the only thing which mattered. Some of them fought as fanatically as any Nazi S.S. man and they had the oddest collection of weapons. Capture by the Germans meant certain death, and they were fully prepared to accept this in order to show that the spirit of France was by no means broken and that many brave hearts had waited for this moment through seemingly unending years of oppression and slavery.

The close of the day brought us to the two adjoining villages of Gouy and Servins just north of Arras, the Company splitting into two parts to garrison these places. Hospitality and kindness were again lavished on us and we were able to spend a comfortable and peaceful night here. Our Echelon again arrived, having travelled a greater distance than ever before.

Orders had now come through that we were to race for the great port of Antwerp, and, even after our recent experiences, this news was greeted rather dubiously and with smiles when I announced it to my order group. Time was to show.

The 2nd of September was the sort of day we had always dreamed of and which we thought could never come true. Our route lay through the factory towns near Lens to Pont-a-Vendin. The tumultuous welcomes we received from the obviously poverty-stricken districts of these towns were most moving, and there could not be a shadow of doubt that they had been living for this day and that, having at last come, they were quite determined to make it the most memorable day of their lives. Our vehicles were heaped high with flowers, fruit and bottles of every imaginable kind of wine and liqueur, including a fair sprinkling of champagne as well. The danger of flying bullets and shell splinters had been temporarily replaced by an almost equally grave peril of flying tomatoes and splintering glass from beer bottles.

Opposition was practically non-existent and we crossed the bridge over the canal at Pont-a-Vendin and turned north to Bauvin, where we halted. 10 Platoon, however, pushed on to the next town, Anneullin, where they were swamped by the vast crowds of hysterically happy people, who thronged the streets and main square. In these situations, the only thing to do was to stay in one's vehicles. Once out of it there was no telling what might happen.

10 Platoon were withdrawn from Anneullin before night came, and we were ordered to hold two bridges across the canal in rather widely separated points. To each of these went a motor platoon and a section of carriers, 11 Platoon and Company H.Q. remaining in Bauvin. Rumours were current that very considerable enemy forces were in the neighbourhood and various alarms developed.

Shortly after midnight the bridge defended by 12 Platoon was attacked by a large force of Germans. Before they came in to the attack they had mortared 12 Platoon's position, and one mortar bomb caused the death of Michael Anderson and Sergt. Macaulay, who had both contributed so much to our success and who were two of the most likeable and able leaders we had. After this disastrous blow, Cpl. Shutz, who had previously been commanding a section, took over command of the Platoon and acted with great coolness and courage. A few Germans succeeded in crossing the bridge and the situation became difficult, causing me to send 11 Platoon to their assistance. Dawn arrived and a troop of the 3rd Royal Tank Regiment's tanks arrived on the scene and did some very useful work in restoring the situation. 10 Platoon had had an undisturbed night at the other bridge, but were unfortunately not in a position to be able to support or help 12 Platoon in any way.

I had hoped that we would have time to clear up this situation, but this was not to be the case. Orders came through that we had to press on towards our ultimate goal, Antwerp, with all possible speed and that anything else was of secondary importance.

So I called in the platoons from their various locations and fixed a rendezvous on the green at Bauvin. I had also obtained permission to have half an hour's grace for reorganization, and then we were to double bank the column and regain our proper place.

We had also to face the loss of three carriers, all of which could probably have been recovered if we had had time, and, coupled with our personnel casualties, the night had provided us with a nasty blow. The remainder of 12 Platoon was hastily reorganized and Sergt. Carr took command of it.

Spirits were soon flying high again, as we once more took the road, regaining our rightful place in the order of march.

Some opposition was met at Seclin, but with the help of the Maquis this was cleared enough to enable us to crack on.

Skirting south of Lille, we reached the border town of Willems; a strange coincidence that our last French village should have named after it our last location in England, Willems Barracks, Aldershot.—

And so farewell to France and the first stage of our liberation mission in Europe. Those of us who had not visited France before the war, felt that we had acquired very little knowledge of the country or its people during our two and a half months' stay there. In Normandy the countryside on the whole was very pleasant, but the last part of our journey had been across very flat, uninteresting terrain, which left us very unimpressed. The people we had only seen and met from a very superficial angle, and there had been no opportunity of really finding out the views and policies of the average Frenchman. They were undoubtedly glad to be freed from the German yoke but how and with what energy they were going to build a new France were questions hard to answer. Four years of occupation had left its mark only too clearly.

Our first impressions of Belgium were very favourable, and the welcomes we received everywhere seemed much warmer and more genuine than those in France.

The first Belgian town of any size we came to was Renaix, and here to our great surprise and amusement we found our A.1. Echelon waiting to tail in behind us. They had taken the wrong turning further back and had raced on, acting as a soft vanguard to our armoured column.

At this time we were catching up and destroying as we swept past them increasing numbers of German horse-drawn columns. And so on to Audenarde, where there was a bit of shooting, which was soon cleared up.

The petrol tanks of our tracked vehicles were almost dry when we stopped just beyond Audenarde for a refuelling halt, giving us time also for a much-needed brew of tea. An unfortunate incident occurred here, however, when a party of Germans drove down a side road into our column and destroyed a tank and a half-track belonging to the Sappers. We had been moving so fast against practically no opposition that a feeling of over-confidence had crept in, and we needed an incident such as this to bring us sharply to our senses and to make us realize that we had not yet won the war completely.

It was almost dark when we moved on again through Alost to Termonde, where we lost our way hopelessly and went round and round the town many times. The very early hour of morning—it was just after midnight—did not prevent the townspeople from turning out and giving us a great welcome. Pyjama-clad men, women and children thronged the streets, and one doubtless well-meaning citizen would persist in firing Very lights into the air, an action which we viewed at first with grave distrust.

At long last, with two hours of darkness still remaining, we turned into some fields on the outskirts of Termonde, having broken all our previous records for a single day's advance. A distance of some ninety miles had been covered, and the knock we had received before setting out on this memorable day was fast receding in our memories, everyone being at the top of their form again. The strain was beginning to tell on our vehicles, however, and we were now down to three carriers in the scout platoon.

The 4th of September was to provide the climax to our historic advance across France and Belgium, a day which none of us will ever forget.

At first light the Company, together with John Dunlop's squadron of the 3rd Royal Tank Regiment, set off with Antwerp as our goal. The remainder of the tanks were to follow later, when we had reported back how we were getting on. John and I, knowing Colonel Silvertop, however, knew that in point of fact they would be close on our heels and not wanting to be left out of the final party.

We raced along the broad highway to Willebroeck and there turned north to Boom. So far we had met no opposition, but a number of prisoners had come in and we showed them the way to go home. As we had feared, the main bridge at Boom was blown and it looked as if we might be held up here for a while, when a civilian approached us, saying he was an engineer and a prominent member of the resistance movement. He volunteered to lead us round to another bridge which was still intact and it was reasonable to hope that if we moved with speed we might prevent it being blown.

So away we went and, to our great satisfaction, we crossed the bridge and immediately sat firmly on either end of it to prevent any desperate Germans from trying to blow it, while the rest of the 3rd Royal Tank Regiment crossed over. We owed a great debt of gratitude to that engineer for his resourcefulness and courage, without which we should never have reached our objective so quickly.

Our goal was now near and we wondered what sort of a fight the Germans would put up for Antwerp. Surely they realized what a wonderful prize it would be for us. But as we left Boom and moved through the cheering throngs all along the broad approaches to the city, there was not a sign of a German anywhere. Then suddenly as we arrived at the city itself shots rang out, Germans began throwing grenades on to us from a window of a high building near us, twenty millimetre guns opened up, and we knew at least that we would have to fight for it. As we dealt swiftly with the scattered and disorganized opposition, we could see ahead of us the main streets of the city densely packed with crowds awaiting us, and this spurred us on in our efforts. Then came the great moment, as we entered the heart of the city, to receive a welcome none of us had ever dreamed was possible. Our vehicles were unable to move and were smothered with people; we were overwhelmed by flowers, bottles and kisses. Everyone had gone mad and we allowed ourselves a few minutes to take stock of the situation. We had to get to the docks at all costs to save them from being destroyed by the Germans, who might by now be getting organized.

Everyone wanted to show us the way and everyone wanted us to go and deal with German pockets all over the place. With the very greatest difficulty we managed to get on the move again, and ploughed our way through to the Scheldt, unfortunately getting separated from the tanks. We then came under fire from the far bank of the Scheldt at the same time as we were engaged in two different street battles on the near side, and I began to wonder whether we should ever see the tanks again. They, however, were equally worried at not having us with them, but it was very difficult to describe over the wireless exactly where we were. A tank was sent to try and contact us, and after some time, to our great relief, a Sherman hove in sight round a corner, running a gauntlet of Germans firing bazookas at it.

The next thing to do was to collect the Company together from the various little battles which were in progress. Our medical truck had unfortunately been knocked out and we had some wounded on our hands, which were shortly afterwards handed over to a local hospital. After a while, however, we became one body again and set off to rejoin the tanks. Civilians were still all over our vehicles and numbers were killed or wounded by the remaining German snipers and machine-gun posts which one was quite likely to meet round any corner. No heed was taken of our repeated warnings, and it was quite impossible to keep our vehicles clear of civilians and at the same time be on the alert ourselves.

The docks were completely undamaged and we spent the rest of the day dealing with the few remaining pockets of resistance and keeping an eye open to see that the dock installations were not sabotaged.

As evening drew on, we all drew in and concentrated with the tanks in a single street, blocking both ends. Hospitality was lavished on us and we were all able to look clean again, as well as at last having time to sit back and have a quiet drink. No untoward incidents occurred that night in our area, which was brightly illuminated by two blazing warehouses two blocks away from us.

And so ended probably the most historic day in any of our lives so far. Only a few weeks before we had been fighting with our backs to the sea in the beachhead and now we were right through France and most of Belgium. In addition, the great port of Antwerp had fallen into our hands intact, which was the greatest prize the Allied armies had yet won in Europe.

The following morning we continued the work of mopping up, and it was during this that our mortar detachment had undoubtedly their "best ever" shoot. The mortars themselves were placed in one of the large squares in the city, where enthusiastic citizens crowded round and began ripping up the pavement to make firm the base plates. Meanwhile, Sergt. Fruin and I had gone down to the bank of the Scheldt, from where we intended to observe. Large parties of Germans had been reported on the far bank and the prospects of targets appeared good. Being unable to see from ground level, we entered a tall bank building on the waterfront and a most obliging lift attendant took us up to the sixth floor. Here we got the most wonderful view of the country on the far side of the river, and one of the first sights that met our eyes was a collection of stationary German transport. We wirelessed back to the mortars to engage this target, and shortly afterwards a salvo of bombs fell among the transport, whereupon some sixty Germans, who must have been taking it easy within the vehicles, leapt out and began milling around in the open, not knowing where to go. The new target was worked out and within a few seconds down came bomb after bomb right into the middle of them, scoring the most direct hits I have ever seen. Hardly a German escaped this murderous hail of bombs, which we went on firing till all the ammunition was exhausted. We had just descended to ground level again when the Germans, who by now had realized that we were using the building as an observation post, began to shell it, but the work was done and we made off in good spirits.

After lunch we were relieved by our infantry brigade and the squadron of tanks and ourselves made our way back through the city to the pleasant suburb of Hemixem, where we rejoined the remainder of the group. Here we had thirty-six hours in which to reorganize ourselves, while supplies were rushed up to enable the great drive to retain its momentum. A lot of work was done and at the same time everyone enjoyed themselves in Antwerp, where fantastic rejoicing went on for days and where one did not need to be introduced to make friends.

Donald Howarth joined us and took over 12 Platoon.

Described by the press as the greatest military motor drive in history, the "great swan" to Antwerp had been packed full of incidents and excitements of all kinds. But though the cost in comparison to what had been achieved was small, we had lost twenty-eight men, who had become casualties in ones and twos all along the way, giving us sad and sobering thoughts to reflect on as well as the gayer ones.

Over-confidence had crept in and we were apt to think that nothing more lay in front of us. The succeeding chapter, however, will soon reveal how we were quickly brought back to our senses and made to realize that much still had to be achieved. There was once again time only for brief rejoicing.

CHAPTER VIII

THE BULL DIVERTS

VAST numbers of Germans had been left behind during our last operation, and we had kept well south of the strongly defended Channel ports. Slower-moving forces were now dealing with these Germans and there was always the very likely possibility that they would drive them back on to us. Accordingly, before we next moved off, several alarming reports came in and caused us to spend one uncomfortable night in particular. But happily nothing came of these threats.

On the 7th of September, we set off again in high spirits to cross the Albert Canal at Merxem, where the 159th Infantry Brigade were to make a bridgehead. Things did not quite go according to plan, however, and the King's Shropshire Light Infantry got cut off in a most unpleasant factory area on the other side of the canal. We waited for several hours, ready to cross and exploit the bridgehead, but the enemy positions turned out to be too strong and the operation had to be abandoned.

For the first time for a very long time the Bull had been halted in his path and had to retrace his steps. So having turned our vehicles round, we once again drove through the city of Antwerp, trying in vain to conceal from the citizens our sense of frustration and disappointment.

In one way this setback had been a good thing. It had brought us right down to earth again and had dispelled our feeling of over-confidence. The war was not over and the sooner we realized it the better.

We spent the rest of the day in our old harbour area at Hemixem, while fresh plans were being made for our future. No time was wasted and early the next morning the 3rd Royal Tank Regiment and ourselves moved off, this time on a "peacetime" march through territory that had already been liberated. Our route lay through Malines and Aerschot to Diest, where we harboured just to the south-east of the town. We were now alongside the Americans, who at this time were suffering from a grave shortage of petrol, and one of our carrier sections was sent off to contact them at Donck.

A bridgehead over the Albert Canal had been in the meantime made by the Guards who had gone across with the 8th Armoured Brigade. This was at Beeringen, and on the 9th September we too crossed the same bridge. On approaching it, however, we saw one of the biggest "brews" we had ever set eyes on, and this turned out to be a long column of supply vehicles of the 8th Armoured Brigade. The enemy had infiltrated back into the area during the night and this was the result of their work. The wooded nature of the country here lent itself admirably to this type of operation, and there was no doubt that the Germans had done the job very thoroughly and skilfully. In addition some enormous slag-heaps dominated the whole area and snipers were still very much in evidence when we crossed the bridge. However, although well within range of their guns, the Germans were not attempting to shell it.

After taking up positions in Beeringen, itself, we were ordered to clear the wooded area to the north of the town, which was where the infiltrating Germans were assumed to be lying up. I split the company into two and, with tanks supporting, the two columns moved through this wooded country. A vast area of woodland was combed through and a fair number of prisoners were taken. The operation was very slow and tiring, as it all had to be done on foot, but we did receive some quite enthusiastic help from an infantry company of the Dutch Army. However, at last all was reported clear and we withdrew to Beeringen, where we took up positions for the night in defence of the town.

And here our historic partnership with the 3rd Royal Tank Regiment temporarily ended. I can never say anything too high in praise of them for their wonderful work whilst we were with them. They were extremely lucky in having in Colonel David Silvertop a leader of the very highest order, who I consider was personally responsible for a great deal of the success the Division had achieved during the plan just ended. He always showed us the greatest consideration and his own personal courage inspired us all. It was accordingly with very great regret that we said farewell to the "wearers of the green," earnestly hoping it would not be long before we resumed our partnership once again.

Nothing untoward occurred that night and the next morning we set off early to join up with "A" Squadron of the 23rd Hussars, from whom we had parted at Laigle just under a fortnight before. All was peaceful until Helchteren, where the leading group became heavily involved and we were looped round to the north, the intention being that we should rejoin the centre line in the rear of the enemy position and so influence the situation.

This manoeuvre proved highly successful and the leading carriers reached the road to find Germans calmly walking up it and a 75 mm. gun facing the wrong way. The enemy were completely taken by surprise and before they could collect their wits had been written off in no uncertain manner. The gun and its crew were also speedily put out of action.

On moving up the road, however, we very soon ran into another position astride the road and this we engaged for the rest of the day. It was held by a considerable number of German paratroopers, very lightly armed and very badly organized, but who fought fanatically, preferring to shoot themselves rather than be taken prisoners. They suffered enormous casualties and the carnage over the whole area was the greatest we had yet witnessed. Donald Howarth, who had been so short a time with us, was killed while assisting a wounded man in his platoon, but otherwise our losses were comparatively light. Darkness fell and we spent the night in a field with the tanks, expecting to be attacked, but once again our fears were unjustified and all was quiet.

The remnants of the paratroopers made off during the night, leaving behind them mines which we found next morning. The position they had occupied, was littered with dead bodies and abandoned equipment, and there was no doubt that they had paid very dearly for the slight delay they had succeeded in imposing upon us.

No further trace of Germans was seen after this during our advance to Petit Brogel, where we got a very warm welcome from the villagers. We had bypassed Peer and were fortunate in this, as while we were waiting at Petit Brogel the remainder of the regimental group moving up through this town met a certain amount of opposition before they got through to us. On their arrival we learnt that Petit Brogel was to become our resting-place for the next few days, and we accordingly set about making ourselves as comfortable as possible.

Our warlike activities here were confined to sending out several patrols on to the line of the Escaut Canal, and nothing of great interest occurred on any of them. A German patrol one night penetrated to Company H.Q., but having thrown a grenade into our area, they were dispersed at high speed by the sentries.

The remainder of our time was spent in resting and reorganizing, the first real break we had had since leaving Laigle. The vast collections of wines, liqueurs and cigars we had collected during our travels were to a large extent consumed during this period, and our loaded transport was accordingly relieved of some of its burden.

On the 17th of September, we moved a couple of miles to Grand Brogel, where we remained for three days, pursuing much the same activities as those at Petit Brogel. Our first "liberty" party went to Brussels, and the first batch of members of the Company who were wounded in Normandy returned to the fold.

Harbert and Breed, who had been taken prisoner in the action at Provin on our way to Antwerp, also found their way back to us, and Harbert told me this story of their adventures in the hands of the Germans.

"We were pulled out of a carrier by the scruffs of our necks like rabbits and taken to a house two miles down the road, where we were very thoroughly searched. Then we were marched a further five miles where we were interrogated. The German Officer who conducted the interrogation spoke excellent English, and his first question was 'Which way did you come over here from England?' I replied that I travelled only at night, and in any case had it been during the day I would not have known as I could not read very well. After a while we were pushed into a cellar for the rest of the night.

"In the morning we joined fourteen other prisoners and started on our march towards Germany. The Germans had very little transport, and what vehicles there were were commandeered by their officers, who drove off in the morning, leaving the other ranks to plod along on their feet and catch them up in the evening.

"For four days we had no food and our only drink was water from four steel helmets, which we were given every evening. On the fifth day a German gave us one tin of meat, which we had to eat with the aid of a pencil, and a cigarette, which was rationed to two puffs a man.

"The next day we were told that if any man escaped the rest would be shot, but in spite of this two men escaped that night. Accordingly the following morning we were lined up against a wall with a machine gun trained on us and with a blanket over our heads. The officer then said: 'You were warned that if any man escaped, the remainder of you would be shot.' I assured him, however, that the two men had not escaped, but had been put on a cart because they were too exhausted to walk. He said no more, but took the machine gun and blanket away and we breathed again.

"Later that day, I said to the rest of the lads, that in view of the morning's affair, it was every man for himself, and that I was going to escape that night.

"In the darkness a cart became conveniently jammed against a telegraph pole and I went forward to assist in extricating it. While the guards were pushing in the front, I pushed from the rear, at the same time looking searchingly around me. To the right was a house and I made a dash for the back of it, raced across several fields and found myself on a stretch of what I later heard was the Albert Canal. I found a small boat and was half-way across when six shots rang out. Cursing my luck, I paddled back to find a large figure on the bank awaiting me. To my relief, I found he was a fellow prisoner from the Reconnaissance Corps, who seeing me escape had rapidly followed suit.

"The two of us hid in a barn alongside a house, concealing ourselves beneath a large pile of potatoes. Here we lay for nineteen hours, and during this time the Germans blew up the bridge over the canal.

"The following afternoon a young girl entered the barn to collect some potatoes and I don't know who was the most shaken, the girl discovering us, or ourselves at being discovered. She fetched her family and with great relief we learnt that the Germans had been pushed back. These people were very kind to us and gave us plenty to eat, a bath and a comfortable bed. Two days later the 15th Scottish Division entered the village and we reported to an officer and were plied with cigarettes and food, eating as we had never eaten before.

"I had no chance of finding out the names of the places we had been through, but I worked out afterwards that I must have walked well over two hundred miles, and my feet were covered with festering blisters. The only food we had had was the one tin of meat between us and a few green potatoes. I had well and truly learnt how the Germans treated their prisoners."

12 Platoon had to be disbanded to make up 10 and 11 for our next operation, which we learnt was to be right flank protection for the drive by 30 Corps through Holland, in conjunction with the great airborne landing which was about to take place.

And so it was to be farewell to Belgium, a country we had taken a great liking to during our short stay in it and whose people we had taken to our hearts. It was easy to see that political strife and much unrest were in store for the Belgians, but their feeling of friendship and gratitude to the British people was quite unanimous, and it impressed us greatly.

CHAPTER IX

WINDMILLS AND CHURCH SPIRES

THE 20th September marked the date of our entry into the third foreign country since leaving the shores of England. I don't think any of us were wildly excited to see what Holland was like, and we crossed the border with a certain amount of doubt and misgiving in our minds, so that the shock and dismay at the countryside in which we were going to live for the ensuing three months might have been much greater if we had been unprepared for it. Such pleasant sights as pretty Dutch girls clad in their national costume as depicted on tourist posters, waiting to greet us on the frontier, were conspicuous by their absence. Instead a collection of very uninteresting and rather suspicious civilians cast occasional glances our way as we passed by. However, even these melted ere long before the overpoweringly winning ways of the Riflemen. I think undoubtedly the language problem was largely to blame, but even this did not prove for long an obstacle to the Rifleman, who appears to have the knack of speaking his own language to foreigners who do not know a word of English and yet who understand him perfectly.

After crossing the Escaut canal at Lille-St-Hubert, we passed through the 3rd British Division, who had made the bridgehead, and pushed on north without incident, arriving in the late afternoon before Heeze. This place we cleared without much difficulty and we settled down for our first night on Dutch soil. Everyone seemed very suspicious here, but I think it was mainly caused by their fear of the Germans returning and taking reprisals. The next day, when we again passed through Heeze, the inhabitants were in a much more friendly and jubilant frame of mind.

Next morning we reached Geldrop, a very friendly place, where during a temporary halt several members of the Company had time to dive into a local barber's alongside our column and have a haircut and shampoo. On we moved again and all went well till, just as we were about to enter Gerwen, the leading two tanks and a carrier were rudely "brewed up." Artillery were called into action and our mortar detachment joined in the fray, causing a number of Germans to make for the nearby woods. Once again an attempt was made to enter Gerwen, this time with a troop of tanks, a section of carriers and 10 Platoon on their feet. At the entry to the village, however, opposition was again met and darkness fell before the attack could be pressed home. We all therefore concentrated into as tight a pocket as we could and prepared to defend ourselves against night intruders, as there was no doubt that the Germans knew exactly where we were. However, nothing unpleasant occurred.

Next morning our vision was obscured by a thick mist, and advancing through this we moved into Gerwen without meeting any opposition. But we saw only too clearly the sites of the guns which had been firing at us the previous day and also the track marks of Panther tanks. No chances were taken, therefore, and we prepared ourselves for a possible counter-attack. James Ramsden, in the meanwhile, had taken a carrier patrol out to see if the bridges across the canal to the north of us were intact. This patrol "swanned" for miles, liberating several villages and meeting no opposition, but reported that the bridges were blown.

The position was now clear—we were hemmed in by canals and no further progress seemed to be likely in the immediate future. Accordingly, we were not surprised when we heard that we were to turn south again back through Geldrop and Heeze to Sonneren, where the Fife and Forfar Yeomanry had succeeded with their infantry battalion in making a bridgehead across the Duc canal.

We sensed immediately, when we crossed the canal the next day, that we were in for a lot of unpleasantness. The signs of bitter fighting in the bridgehead showed that the Germans did not appear to be prepared to let us have our own way. At Asten we passed through the Fife and Forfars, and once we were out of the town mortars opened up at our column, happily scoring no hits at all. Ommel was reached and we occupied it, the Germans having pulled out, leaving a fair number of dead behind. They had been employing cavalry in this area and a large number of dead horses were also littering the place. On attempting to probe farther forward the leading tank was knocked out, and so we consolidated in Ommel before deciding how we were going to get on. Hell was then let loose and the village came in for shelling and mortaring, the like of which we had not seen since Normandy. The Germans were using huge rocket mortars, and one of these landed beside our stretcher-bearer half-track, transferring it into a mass of twisted metal and rendering it quite unrecognizable as a vehicle. A sad loss to us was the death of the driver, Clermont, a Frenchman, who had joined us early after the fall of France, but who had never had the opportunity to see the realisation of his dreams—his liberated home in Northern France. Three of our half-tracks were destroyed and we had other personnel casualties, but on the credit side we had the satisfaction of inflicting quite heavy casualties on the enemy, who tried to infiltrate back into the village.

In addition to our Company casualties, we all suffered a great loss that unhappy day when our Padre, Jeff Taylor, who since the Normandy days had instilled faith and hope into so many of us, was killed in our very lines while he was endeavouring to locate some helpless children who had been wounded during the shelling. His loss was felt a great deal by all of us, and it seemed so unjust that such a saintly and good person should be taken from us just when we needed him most.

We remained in the village for the night, very spread out on the ground, hoping against hope that we would not be disturbed. In the middle of the night, however, a stentorian voice rang through the darkness and we could not think what was happening. All was well, however, and it was merely our tame "Dr. Goebbels," consisting of loudspeakers mounted on a vehicle, appealing to the Germans in the neighbourhood to come in and give themselves up, promising in return food, rest, and all the other attractions of a prisoner-of-war cage. There was no response whatever to this appeal, and once again we settled down in our snug ditches to a few more hours of sleep.

Light came and all was quiet, the enemy having pulled back during the night, as so often happened. Many times the close of a hard day's fighting had come making us feel perhaps a little despondent, mainly due to weariness; then a few hours' sleep and next morning all our despondency had vanished, enabling us to begin off the day again with fresh hope and energy. That morning at Ommel was certainly no exception to the rule, and after a few quiet hours in the village we moved on to Deurne through villages already cleared and entered the town without incident. However, as we were parking the Company H.Q. transport, one of the mortar carriers, to our great surprise and dismay, was very rudely "brewed up" by a gun which was shortly afterwards severely dealt with. After having been in the town for a short while, the Germans began shelling it sharply, but no one was hit and it was only of nuisance value.

An uneventful day followed, during which we moved a few miles north from Deurne, spending the next night in the open in pouring rain in a most unattractive setting. We had now cut the German escape route from the west and so had to keep on our toes in case any tried to fight their way through us. This had actually happened several times during the day in another sector, and one such incident brought the grievous news to us all of the death of Colonel David Silvertop. We had lost in him, as well as a very great commander, a personal friend who was admired and greatly liked by all ranks of the Company.

A few miles farther on, brought us, on the 26th September, to Judiths Hoeve, where we settled down with "A" Squadron for a pleasant week's rest. Although remaining officially operational here, the danger of direct attack was very small and we were able to relax considerably. A few shells came over one night and there was the chance of the odd German patrol putting in an appearance during the hours of darkness; otherwise all was quiet. "Liberty" trucks were sent off to Helmond, where there were cinemas and baths, the remaining time being devoted to rest, cleaning and reorganization. We also had a very successful concert party, the talent being selected from members of the Company and Squadron, as well as, on the more serious side, some very well-attended evening services in the barn we had commandeered.

The sad news had come through of the failure of the heroic attempts by the gallant 1st Airborne Division at Arnhem, and no one quite knew what would happen next. At any rate it looked painfully obvious that our last hope of finishing the war before the winter set in had vanished and the prospect of the winter months in this bleak countryside was not inviting.

The only landmarks anywhere for miles were windmills and church spires. Both of these objects were disliked intensely by the Germans and came in for some really cruel punishment during the campaign in Holland, windmills often completely vanishing into thin air and church spires rapidly assuming the appearance of sieves. The builders of windmills and the fashioners of church spires should be kept fully employed for years, restoring Holland's landmarks.

We were roused from our inactivity on the 3rd October and ordered to proceed to Meijel, a "no-man's land" village right out in the blue, and to the south of Deurne. I commanded Meijelforce, which came under the direct command of the 11th Armoured Division and consisted of the following components: "G" Company, a troop of tanks of 23rd Hussars, a troop of armoured cars of the Inns of Court, a troop of 25-pdr. guns, a section of the Light Field Ambulance and some machine and anti-tank guns from "E" Company. This very mixed bag formed an extremely far-flung outpost of the Holland line. The village was very battered and straggling, which made it hard to defend, and I quite honestly hesitate to think what might have happened if an attack of any strength had been made against us. Still, here we were and we had to make the best of it. During the daytime sporadic mortaring and shelling went on most of the time, to which we replied, but the danger of enemy attack was very small. At night, however, far from wondering whether anything was going to happen, it was a question of waiting for something actually *to* happen. Three nights we spent in this eerie village, each night seeming to last for an age. The first night an enemy patrol approached our positions, but made off without firing a shot. The second night a party of Germans reached the vehicles of 10 Platoon, but were fired on by the drivers, a grenade being thrown at them in return. Some, however, had managed to infiltrate into the main street of the village, and Francis McGinnis, our anti-tank gun commander, had a bullet through his tin hat which miraculously only grazed his head.

By the third night we were all extremely "trigger conscious" and this time the Germans chose as their objective our 25-pdr. gunners, who were lying a short way back from us. Just before dawn on a given signal they made a three-sided attack. One of these attacks was directed against our carrier section which was with the guns, and here the Germans had a hot reception. The gunners fared disastrously, losing two officers amongst their casualties as well as a gun and a vehicle—an unfortunate ending to our stay here, which made us even more pleased to welcome the arrival of a new Meijel-force later in the day and to take our leave of this singularly uninviting village. Still, we might have fared a great deal worse, as it was not very long afterwards that the Germans launched an attack against the village with strong tank and infantry forces. And I think that, with the meagre forces we had at our disposal, we should have well and truly "had it" if we had been there at that time.

While we had been at Meijel, German patrols had been laying mines in our area at Judiths Hoeve, and our first notification of this activity, was when James Ramsden, Donald Sudlow and a troop leader of "A" Squadron proceeded out on a reconnaissance in a carrier and went up on a mine, the troop leader being killed and Donald and James badly concussed. More mines were found nearby and were speedily neutralized.

One morning also just after dawn we saw an abandoned truck about a hundred yards down the road from us, belonging to an artillery regiment. The occupants, who were on their way back with N.A.A.F.I. supplies for their regiment, had been ambushed by a German patrol, who drove the truck on until one of the petrol tanks was empty. Not knowing how to change over tanks, they had abandoned the truck, left several mines in it, and made off back to their own lines. The N.A.A.F.I. stores were almost intact and we luckily reached the truck before the local civilians had a chance to loot it. Brushing temptation aside, we drove it to Company H.Q., put a guard over it, and got word through to its rightful owners. An officer arrived later in the day to claim it and we handed it over to him complete except for a few bottles of gin and whisky, which we retained as a small salvage fee.

We sent out several patrols to try and ambush the mine-layers, but had no luck. This was our only operational activity and life for the next week consisted once more of rest and recreation. The first official short leave to Brussels began and some of our Normandy warriors set out to make the scheme a big success. The Company and Squadron were still living together, sharing work and entertainments alike, and a very pleasant spirit of friendship and cooperation existed between them.

The 7th United States Armoured Division came through us to set about clearing the strip of country in front of us up to the west bank of the Maas, but various complications and changes of plan occurred and a few days later they retraced their steps and the job was left to the 3rd British Division to undertake. I am afraid we were rather critical of them at the time, but they showed their true worth some months later in the Ardennes, where they put up a great show. They were very good customers, however, at this time for various trophies we had picked up during our travels, Lugers and S.S. daggers appearing particularly attractive to them. They paid ready cash if required, but in most cases the barter system was resorted to, and various members of the Company now began appearing in garments of all descriptions. An American officer summed up the whole situation in a nutshell. "You English," he said "are fighting for freedom, the Russians are fighting for Russia and we Americans are fighting for souvenirs."

The 16th of October saw our next operation commence—the clearing of the enemy in the "Venray pocket" west of the River Maas. 12 Platoon had been re-formed and Barry Keitley-Webb arrived to take command of it, and so we set off again fairly well up to strength as well as rested. The weather was atrocious, and the mud made the going very difficult, when we crossed the canal. No enemy were met for some time, but mines were plentiful, and a party on foot had to sweep a path the whole way to the village of Haag, where we took up a position for the night.

The next day we tried pushing on towards Weverslo, but we soon ran into demolitions and the going was appalling. The enemy were reacting fairly strongly to our movements, too, and were shelling us, adding to the discomfort of the mud and pouring rain. A scissors bridge was eventually sent to us and with the aid of this we managed to get over the first water obstacle. 12 Platoon, leading the advance on foot, were fired on from Weverslo, but the fire was quickly neutralized and they went on. After another couple of hundred yards, however, three tanks and a flail, which we also had with us, became well and truly bogged, and there seemed to be no hope of extricating them. Darkness was coming on and we merely had to content ourselves with staying where we were. 12 Platoon and a section of carriers sat with the "bogged" tanks, 11 Platoon round the scissors bridge and the remainder of the Company still at Haag. Altogether, a most unpleasant and unfruitful day. Our casualties from the fairly constant shelling had not been heavy, however, but everyone was drenched to the skin and it continued to pour with rain all night.

Enemy resistance on the front was definitely cracking, however, and this enabled us to reach the village of Heide next day without much difficulty. In the village itself was a mass of abandoned equipment, and 10 Platoon collected in a lot more prisoners in the evening. The civilians told us that the Typhoons had put in an appearance the previous day and this had very definitely decided the wavering morale of the German troops in the neighbourhood.

We had now lost contact with the enemy, and on the 19th October, we entered without opposition the large village of Leunen, a name which will always live in our memories. Here we were ordered to halt and consolidate, which was disappointing in many ways, as we really felt we had the Germans on the run. This was in fact the case, and we later heard that the whole of this operation conducted by 8th Corps had to be held up to enable the offensive in Western Holland to take place. The supply situation had not yet been built up to sufficient strength to enable the two operations to be conducted simultaneously, and we had to be the ones to suffer.

All was quiet at Leunen until we had settled ourselves well in, when the enemy began to rain down on us shells and mortar bombs in no uncertain manner. We occupied half of the village, and for this purpose were allotted a machine gun and an anti-tank gun platoon of "E" Company, so that we were fairly strong on the ground.

The following day, however, "B" Squadron and "F" Company moved elsewhere and we were left to defend the whole village, which was not such an inviting proposition. I accordingly decided to form a platoon from the Echelon and cooks, fitters, storemen, clerks, and everyone we could lay hands on were thrown into the line under the command of James Ramsden. This gallant band of warriors did great work in their most unpleasant position, and although I don't suppose they will admit it, at times enjoyed it all. I fervently hoped, however, that none of the cooks would be taken prisoner, thus enabling the German propaganda service to put out the story that the British were so short of men that they had to employ the Army Catering Corps in the line.

We remained in these positions for the next five days, being shelled and mortared the whole time and on one occasion bombed in addition. Considering however, the number of direct hits on the houses occupied by us, our casualties were very light. German patrolling was fairly active, on one occasion a couple of Germans appearing outside the joint Company-Squadron H.Q., but they were duly dispatched on their way. Another patrol met a hail of fire from the Echelon platoon and rapidly made off. The first day the shelling was so uncannily accurate that we felt sure that someone in the village had some form of communication with the Germans. We accordingly had the civilians evacuated and as a result, although the shelling did not decrease in intensity, it was definitely not so accurate.

The civilians were allowed to take what livestock they could with them, and after they had gone any left behind became ours, so the feeding at any rate began to look up, if nothing else did.

Trip-flares were laid everywhere and one night, as a section of 10 Platoon were just about to open fire on a figure which had been illuminated by one of these flares, they saw just in time that it was a girl who was approaching. A certain amount of sympathy was extended to her, but we always had our suspicions due to her rather strange behaviour, and she later turned out to be a spy who had tried to infiltrate into our lines.

Another lighter incident concerning trip-flares which might well have been disastrous was the occasion one night when our indomitable Sergt. Carr went out to lay one in front of 10 Platoon's position. The flare went off in his hand and a section who had not been put in the picture opened fire on him. Whereupon Sergt. Carr slowly turned round and said "It's lucky you are all such bloody bad shots," and then went quietly on setting up a fresh one.

And so life went on, humour again coming out on top on many occasions. Company H.Q. resorted to writing verse and the two short odes which I am going to quote represented our trend of thought in between the daily shelling. The first one was composed by Jeremy Taylor, who was now commanding "A" Squadron, and ran as follows :—

> Though they "stonk" us day and night,
> Till the groups are dead with fright,
> And they infiltrate with "S" mines to array,
> The Third British shell us too—
> We don't like that, would you ?—
> We never show the feather at the capital.
>
> Now we've packed in very tight,
> 'Cos to guard ourselves at night
> We've had to use the operators too ;
> So at keeping watch we slave,
> Though to "kip" is all we crave—
> We never show the feather at the capital.
>
> We lie down on the floor
> Behind shutters and closed door,
> You'd think to see us we were rather scared,
> But we haven't got a bed.
> And we work all day, 'tis said—
> We never show the feather at the capital.
>
> With the picture we're *au fait*,
> Tho' it's pretty hard I'll say
> When no one ever tells us anything ;
> When stuff's flying everywhere
> Our Dignity's still there,
> 'Cos we never show the feather at the Capital.

The second, composed by Kingsmill was an ode to the Commander-in-Chief, written shortly after he had been promoted to Field-Marshal :—

> When all the world's a rumble
> And cordite fills the air
> And houses crash and crumble
> (How vertical my hair !)
> And "Minnies" round the corner
> And Siegfried guns give play,
> Then give three cheers for Monty—
> We're being "stonked" today.
>
> When shells come round us falling,
> A strange disease I'll vouch
> Appears, the symptoms being
> A tendency to crouch,
> A swelling of the eardrums
> And passion shown for clay.
> Let's give three cheers for Monty—
> We're being "stonked" today.
>
> I'm not exactly partial
> To whines which fill the air,
> But He's been made Field-Marshal,
> So what have I to care.
> If mighty Sunray's cosy
> In caravan so gay,
> Then give three cheers for Monty—
> We're being "stonked" today.

On the 25th October, we were relieved from the "Bomb Happidrome," as we had now nicknamed our area, by the Monmouths of our infantry brigade and we moved back a few miles to Usselstein, where we occupied three farmhouses, from which the civilians had been evacuated. German patrols were apt to intrude into the area by night, but we ourselves were not troubled and the form was to surround the farmhouse with trip-flares and live comfortably inside. Our pork and chicken supplies were still ample and we fed like kings.

We sent out several patrols at night and from one of these 10 Platoon returned with a prisoner. Otherwise our activities were confined to some much-needed maintenance, re-organization and rest.

This peaceful period lasted for a week, the only real "flap" occurring when the Germans launched their small-scale counter-offensive to the south of us, retaking Meijel and getting close enough to Deurne to shell our Echelon. The 15th Scottish Division rushed back from the west of Holland to deal with the threat and, as invariably happened, this great and very hard-worked division mastered the situation. Things would have been very uncomfortable for us if the Germans had retaken Deurne, as roads in this appallingly flat and marshy bit of country were few and far between and our only supply route ran through the town.

Then back we went to rejoin "A" Squadron in our old area at Leunen, where conditions had not altered one bit whilst we had been away. The village looked even more of a shambles than before. Our stay this time, though, was only one of two days, and on the 4th November we were relieved by the 5th Battalion Coldstream Guards from the Guards Armoured Division.

The change-over this time was done in order to give us a week's complete rest and we moved north to a pleasant little place called Hathert, a few miles south of Nijmegen. Here there was no sign of war whatever—no damaged houses, no shell holes and no noise; it was a most welcome change. The Guards Armoured Division, which we had joined for the time being, was most hospitable and no effort was spared to make our stay with them an enjoyable one. Cinemas, E.N.S.A. shows, football, baths and clubs were all laid on and we benefited enormously from this week. Reinforcements arrived and the scout platoon was able to form a third carrier section for the first time since leaving Laigle. With these reinforcements, too, came Neil Hughes-Onslow, enabling us to have a spare officer, a luxury we had never enjoyed before.

After all this, the prospect of returning to Leunen was not at all pleasant, but it had to be faced and the 11th of November saw us back in our old haunts again. We had swopped positions with "H" Company, however, and were now in an area considerably less unpleasant from the point of view of shelling. But we could not have things all our way and our living conditions were here very much worse than before. Instead of houses, which although somewhat battered were nevertheless quite comfortable inside, most of the Company lived in dugouts in our new position. Great effort and enterprise were put into these, however, and some of them were remarkably well appointed and comfortable. The weather and mud were appalling and we had to resort to "Weasels" to get up our supplies. Suitable and welcome clothing in the form of gum-boots and leather jerkins arrived up in good supply, so we might have been a great deal worse off than we actually were.

Eventually on the 19th of November we said goodbye to Leunen for good, and no sorrowful glances were cast back as this nightmarish place faded into the distance out of our sight but not out of our memories. This time our relieving force were a battalion of the Warwicks whom we had not seen since the famous day they relieved us on Bas Perier in Normandy. They had had a rough passage in the meantime and very few familiar faces remained amongst them.

Back again we went to Usselstein, but this time we expected to be there only a very short time to enable us to get ready for operation "Nutcracker," which was really a continuation of the task we had left unfinished at Leunen a month before. Once more we were accommodated in farmhouses, and all was quiet, except for one morning when, for no apparent reason, fifteen shells landed in our area, twelve of them fortunately being duds.

On the 22nd November orders for "Nutcracker" came through. The staffs had not had much to do recently and they celebrated their return to activity by issuing the most detailed plans and orders we had ever had. Air photographs were available, too, and we were able to study and get a very clear picture of the terrain across which we were going to move. The weather and mud were still atrocious and the prospects were that everything would get bogged. Altogether it looked to be going to be a most uncomfortable battle, to say the least of it. We were to be ready to move early next morning and having given out all my orders I sat down to play Monopoly for the evening with my headquarters personnel.

In the middle of this game a message was brought in to me which had just come over the 'phone. This contained the amazing news that the Infantry Brigade had already taken our objective and that the 15th Scottish Division were in Horst. It was incredible and it took some time to sink in before an enormous sigh of relief was heaved by all. Such a thing had never happened to 11th Armoured Division before, and the Basher decided that this was definitely an excuse for digging deeper into the rum issue.

We had had a lot of reinforcements from England, who had not yet really been in action, and this seemed to be an excellent time to get down to some training. Accordingly, a programme was worked out for the following week, but, as always happened, just as it began a message came through that we were to be ready to move the next day to take over a sector of the line on the River Maas, north of Venlo.

I took the platoon commanders with me to see our area, where I was told we would find a battalion of the 15th Scottish Division who had just finished clearing it. However, we walked for miles and saw not a trace of a Scotsman. We reached the banks of the river and, having met no Germans on the way, we assumed that the area was clear, although we had no real proof of it whatsoever. I decided that we would have a strong-post on the river bank and the rest of us would sit back in Gunhof, where, although cramped, there was cover for everyone. The floods were very high and the only way to our advance post was along a causeway. As our first party were moving out along this we were horrified to see the causeway suddenly collapse, four carriers being marooned in the floods. The crews remained with them all night and by the next morning the depth of the channel between ourselves and the carriers was five feet. Across this channel one of the "E" Company machine-gunners gallantly swam. A footbridge was then hastily constructed, but that brought us no nearer to recovering the carriers. It was decided that they would have to be recovered from the other side, which was unfortunately under observation of the Germans from the far bank of the Maas. So there was no alternative but to make it a night operation and accordingly plans were made for a bulldozer to be loaned from the sappers the following night.

It was bright moonlight when we heard a "clanking" in the distance which gradually grew louder and louder and then began getting faint again. An unpromising start had been made as the bulldozer took the wrong turning and arrived the wrong side of the floods. So off it set again, making an appalling noise, and eventually arrived at the right place. The Germans that night either were deaf or else they were short of ammunition. The noise we made was frightening, but all the carriers were rescued without any interference at all. The party of sappers and Johnny Maidlow's helpmates had well and truly earned the rum which always miraculously appeared on these occasions.

Otherwise nothing much of interest happened during our week in this area. The platoons used to take it in turns to sit on the river bank in a very comfortable farmhouse and there was very little German activity on the other side of the river. The Maas was very swollen and it would have been a very hazarduous operation to try and cross it in a rowing boat at this time.

On the 6th of December the Inns of Court arrived to take over from us and we moved back to what was advertised as a rest area at Melderslo, a small village near Horst, but was in fact nothing more than a few scattered barns. I am afraid our standard of living and comfort had been fairly high up to now, and it was probably good for us to see how some of our more unfortunate brethren lived. To cap our discomfort a most unfortunate fire broke out at Company H.Q. which was brought under control after some very gallant fire-fighting. This occurred after dark and to facilitate the extinguishing of it we lit up the area with headlights. The sequel to this floodlight display came a short while later when shells began landing in the area, and our infantry brigade H.Q. who were very near us, naturally blamed us for the whole affair.

A week dragged slowly by at Melderslo and we were quite relieved at the end of it to hear that we were once again going up to the line on the Maas, this time to take over from the Herefords, who were going to be "lucky" enough to come back to the "rest" area. We were getting to know the Maas pretty well by now, and this new stretch of river we moved to was just as dull and uninteresting as the previous ones. However, the billets in Houthuizen were good, all civilians having been evacuated and we made ourselves very comfortable. Life was the same as usual and consisted of the odd man keeping an eye open during the day time, with more precautionary measures being taken at night. The Germans on the other side of the river were again very quiet, contenting themselves with firing an occasional rifle shot or sending over a few mortar bombs to remind us that they were still there. Our own mortar detachment, aggressive as ever, amused themselves by dumping all their available bombs on the village of Lomm, which was immediately opposite us on the far bank of the river. They never considered that they had had a really good shoot unless a hail of shells came back in reply, and so we used to try and find a place for them as far away from us as possible.

After a couple of days here, really first-class news came through. The Armoured Regiments from whom we had been divorced since Leunen were going back to Belgium to refit with the new Comet tanks and we were going back with them. It seemed almost too good to be true—to go to an area hundreds of miles from the nearest Germans. Surely something would happen to dash our hopes to the ground. But all was well and so on the night of the 16th of December, having been relieved for the third time this campaign by our old friends the Warwicks, we started off on our long trek to Poperinghe, all being in tremendous form. We were going to have a "slap up" Christmas and really enjoy ourselves.

Little did we know what fate had in store for us.

CHAPTER X

NO TURKEYS FOR CHRISTMAS

It felt novel and strange leaving the battle front in Holland, and I can well remember, on arriving at a certain place, working out that we were now beyond the range of the biggest German guns. And this time it was not for a mere week's rest. It might possibly be for several months and it was not going to be pleasant returning again after all that time. So it was with somewhat mixed feelings that we moved on all through the night towards our distant Utopia. After a while, forward area precautions were relaxed—first side-lights on our vehicles were permitted, then headlights and we even obtained sanction to light open fires for a very welcome "brew." Helmond, Eindhoven, Bourg Leopold, Beeringen and Diest flashed by, and dawn saw us approaching Louvain. By this time, the column was well and truly spread out—some vehicles had gone the wrong way and others had fallen by the wayside, so we paused a while here to try and collect ourselves together and also to have a hurried breakfast. Belgian hospitality sprang to the fore once again and houses and kitchens were soon thrown open to us, enabling plates of egg and bacon to be produced in record quick time.

On we went again via the Brussels by-pass—so near and yet so far to the playground of the Second Army—to Alost and Audenarde, bringing us back memories of the early September days when we were streaming along the same highway, in the opposite direction, bound for Antwerp.

Soon we reached the great battle-fields where our fathers had fought in World War number one, which had now as a contrast become areas used for refitting and resting. Our route ran through Menin and Ypres and, passing under the great Menin Gate, I tried to conjure up in my imagination what these towns and the countryside around them must have looked like some thirty years previously. Here the war had gone on month after month with hardly any gain to either side. What a contrast it was to this 1944 campaign, where in the space of six months we had travelled hundreds of miles and still had hundreds more to go.

Poperinghe came into view and our first impressions were not wholly favourable. It looked a dirty and untidy place, full of cheap cafes, but we were soon to know that it was a town with a heart of gold. The spirit of the British Army in 1914-18 lived on in Poperinghe and the lapse of time between the two wars had made no difference to these kind and hospitable people, who gladly accepted us into their houses like long lost friends. "Tubby" Clayton's Talbot House, the foundation stone of "Toc H," acted also as a link between the two generations of soldiers, both fighting the same common enemy in the cause of freedom and democracy.

There was no doubt in any of our minds now that we were going to have the time of our lives and a Christmas which would live long in our memories. The next days were spent in settling in and sorting ourselves out. Our vehicles were all emptied and cleaned, blanco and brasso reared their ugly heads again, and front-line life rapidly faded into the background.

An unfortunate incident occurred, however, our first evening, when a petrol tanker containing six hundred gallons arrived to replenish our thirsty transport. The driver dropped his inspection lamp, which fused, and the resultant spark was enough to start the greatest conflagration we or the local inhabitants had ever witnessed. People began emptying their houses all around and at one time it looked as if it might spread over a vast area, but the local fire brigade arrived and the prospects looked brighter. It was not long though, before we realized that the local firemen had evidently not dealt with a fire for a very long time and we accordingly had to wrest the apparatus from their hands. This did not prove a popular move and we now had not only to fight the fire, but also the Belgian firemen. After many anxious moments, however, the fire was got under control, but not before it had destroyed a warehouse, an office building and one of our own three-ton lorries. In addition, some well-meaning people in an adjacent house where I lived had thrown all my kit out of my bedroom window into the garden, where it had been systematically looted by the civilians. So ended a disastrous evening and we feared that it would be some time before we could live down the bad impression we must have created.

Our Christmas celebrations were well and truly planned when the bombshell fell. Rundstedt had started on his last desperate gamble, catching the Americans unawares in the Ardennes, but, being so far away from the battlefront, this did not disturb us unduly. We had been told so many times by the Intelligence experts that Germany had very little armour left, so we assumed this to be another local counter-offensive. None of us ever had the faintest idea of the magnitude of the weight of armour Rundstedt had been able to amass during the time we had all been sitting peacefully on the Maas, and it came as a rude shock to us to say the least of it.

At seven o'clock in the morning of the 20th of December I was awakened by the guard commander coming into my bedroom. He informed me that I was to be at an order group at a quarter to eight. No reasonable commander ever had an order group at that hour if it was not necessary and so, climbing out of my very comfortable bed, I silently swore and prepared myself to hear the worst.

A sleepy and rather liverish collection of officers foregathered at a quarter to eight at Battalion Headquarters, and we were told to be ready to move at eleven o'clock. No details of our destination were known, but it was fairly obvious in which direction it lay.

Every single thing had been taken off our vehicles and put into stores, and the Company were scattered all over the place, being billeted in ones and twos in private houses. So by the time I was able to give out my orders and everyone knew what was happening, it worked out that we had just over a couple of hours in which to pack up. Still, despite the bitter disappointment felt by all of us, everyone set to with tremendous energy, and the job was done in far less time than I had ever dared to hope.

Orders were given that on no account were the civilians to be told of what we were going to do, but as always seemed to happen, they knew exactly what was going on and what our future intentions were. Hasty farewell parties were thrown in every house and the civilians seemed determined to make sure that we should not forget them. We had only been in the place for three nights and yet scores of firm friendships had been made, many of which live to this day. No town ever before or ever since had given us such a warm and spontaneous welcome or lavished on us such genuine hospitality.

Our armoured regiments were in a far worse plight than ourselves. They had handed in nearly all their Sherman tanks and were standing by for the new Comet tanks to arrive. So they were going to have to be transported to Brussels, where they would collect some more Shermans and motor straight on to the battle.

Accordingly we were going to be sent on ahead and our armoured friends were to join us at the earliest possible moment.

At a quarter to twelve came the order to move and our long columns of half-tracks and carriers began slowly threading their way through the narrow streets of Poperinghe, once more on the road to battle. The local populace turned out almost to a man to wave farewell to us. It was only "au revoir" we hoped, as the idea was firm in our minds that it might only be a matter of days before we would be back again and this helped somewhat to lessen the blow which had befallen us.

Nightfall found us on the outskirts of Brussels, where we were met and informed of our destination. The drive through, or rather round, the city was a nightmare, with vehicles swanning off in the wrong direction in the pitch darkness. Flying bombs were heard spluttering everhead and several hurtled down on Brussels that night. However, we eventually arrived just south of the city at the village of Overische, where we laid our weary heads to rest in a disused convent.

Signs of the alarm and despondency caused by the German offensive were already evident. Reinforcement Holding Units were all standing-to manning road blocks, and a strange assortment of clerks from Headquarters in Brussels were at action stations. Meanwhile in the city itself the "Whitehall Warriors" were packing their bags and preparing to evacuate themselves, and probably their girl friends too, to safer climes.

This tense atmosphere was accentuated early next morning when, without any warning, some shells fell in the village, and visions of S.S. Panzer divisions streaming towards us came into our minds. However, no one ever discovered the origin of these shells, and we could only assume that they came from an odd German armoured car "on the swan" and out to make a nuisance of itself.

Orders now came through for us to proceed to Charleroi and there to contact the headquarters of a mysterious formation called "R Force," who it appeared were the only troops between us and the advancing Panzer armies. When I describe "R Force" as mysterious, I do not wish to belittle them in any way—it was merely our ignorance which caused us to be unaware of their existence. Actually they had been behind the scenes in many ventures since D Day.

We proceeded to Charleroi with a certain amount of caution as no one was able to give us any idea whatever of the position at the battlefront, and for all we knew we might easily have run straight into a hostile column. Our destination however, was reached without any incident and we found the gallant "R Force" H.Q., who were able to give us a rough idea of what was happening and of what our future was going to be. The main thrust of the German S.S. Panzer Army appeared to be directed on Liège and that of the 5th Panzer Army on Namur and Dinant. There appeared at that time to be nothing very formidable to stop the Germans reaching the Meuse, although there were still some very stout-hearted American pockets holding out on the far side of the river, which were disrupting the communications of the Nazis; Bastogne being the main one of these. "R Force" were holding the stretch of river between Namur and Givet with a "scratch" collection of sappers and a handful of very antique armoured cars and Sherman tanks, manned by crews who had long since bade farewell to active service. This strange collection of arms were in great heart and would have fought valiantly, but they could hardly have hoped to do more than slightly delay the armoured forces of the enemy, had they reached them.

The 29th Armoured Brigade was to take over this stretch of river from "R Force" and was to be split into the usual three parts, each consisting of an armoured regiment and a motor company. "G" Company and our old friends the 3rd Royal Tank Regiment, with whom we were delighted to be again, were to be in the centre at Dinant.

I went on ahead with James Ramsden to get things sorted out there before the Company arrived, and having reached the historic old fortress town of Namur, we turned south to motor alongside the river to Dinant. What a delightful change this part of the Meuse was from the lower reaches we knew so well in Holland. The scenery here was lovely and it made one long to see it during the summer weather. For once anyway we were going to fight in a pleasant part of the world; the people, too, seemed so friendly and appeared delighted to see signs of the British Army approaching.

Scenes of the utmost confusion greeted us in Dinant itself. American columns were going first this way and then that way, refugees were beginning to appear on the roads and rumours of every kind were rife. Stationed in the actual town besides "R Force" appeared to be a platoon of American infantry, a company of American police and a large detachment of American Air Service Corps. Co-ordination of command was non-existent, so I decided that the only thing to do was to plan the defence as if I only had a company and then race round and co-opt the help of all these assorted units.

My headquarters was in a pleasant little hotel, which we completely took over, allowing, however, two rather mysterious women, who appeared to be looking after the place, to remain, whereupon people rushed up to tell us that these women were fifth columnists and that there was a vast quantity of "black market" champagne in the cellar. This interested us considerably and so on the first opportunity a party descended to the cellar to investigate. Nothing was found and we thought no more of the matter. Later, however, we were mortified to hear that closer investigation had revealed the presence of a false wall. Behind this was all the champagne, which we could have put to very good use during the ensuing weeks.

The dining-room made a first-class operations room, and the feverish activity which went on inside it at this time gave it the appearance of at least a Corps H.Q.

Having fixed my own positions, I set forth to contact the commanders of the various American forces. First to the Platoon on the bridge, commanded by the most gigantically tall Sergeant, without a vestige of sense of humour, but who appeared determined to fight to the end in defence of the bridge, and was most willing and anxious to co-operate with me. Next to the company of American military police, commanded by a Captain Trotter, a most genial soul who answered every question I asked him by the phrase "Goddammit, you bet." He had been a regular soldier in the Engineers for many years and was now obviously too old for front-line service. Although we had many laughs at his expense, we had a very great affection for him and he and his men would have done anything for us.

The commander of the Air Service Corps, whom I next visited, was quick to point out that his unit was entirely non-combatant, but he expressed a great willingness to come under my command, and assured us that he would help us all he could. Very shortly afterwards their entertainments officer arrived at my headquarters to invite us to a show, and I also had an invitation to Christmas dinner in their Mess. They certainly had no idea as to the gravity of the situation, which was in many ways a very good thing.

The Company had by now arrived and the platoons settled down to make strong-points of their positions. Order was beginning to appear out of chaos and I did at least know that, as far as operations were concerned, I was in command of all forces at Dinant.

The bridge over the Meuse had been prepared for demolition and all that it was necessary to do was to press a button and up it would go. This was the most appalling responsibility of all. If the bridge went up, all sorts of people would be stranded the other side and I wondered what on earth I would do if the Germans ever broke through and tried to rush the defences.

Evening came and we heard with great relief the distant rumble of tanks, which signalled the approach of the first squadrons of the 3rd Royal Tank Regiment. We now felt we were fairly secure, and although an enormous amount of sorting out remained to be done, the Dinant crossing would now present a very reasonable obstacle to the German advance.

The night passed without incident and next day the remainder of the 3rd Royal Tank Regiment arrived and remained on the high ground a few miles behind us. The situation was definitely beginning to take shape and it looked extremely probable that one of the 5th Panzer Army's groups would be directed on the crossing at Dinant. A squadron of tanks and some of our carriers went forward on patrol, but had nothing to report however. A railway bridge was found to be unguarded and this meant sending off 11 Platoon, which Neil Hughes-Onslow had just taken over, to cope with it. We had, however, been strengthened by three platoons of the support company so we were still reasonably strong on the ground.

Great volumes of traffic, mostly American, were still crossing the bridge, and the refugee problem was getting a little troublesome. The Germans were trying out the fifth column trick again and we had to scrutinize very carefully everyone's papers before letting them through.

Reports of the enemy came flooding in from all quarters, some entirely false and most of them grossly inaccurate. My headquarters was packed all day with people either volunteering or seeking information, and by midday we were almost exhausted and our replies were sometimes curt to say the least of it. We had eventually to put up a notice on the door restricting visits to a maximum duration of five minutes, and even this did not seem to ease our burden. The "star" caller of the day was an American full Colonel who had been sent from S.H.A.E.F. to quote his own words "to make absolutely sure that the various commanders in Dinant know who is responsible for the bridge and for the blowing of the bridge." This he must have repeated to me a dozen times, adding "I want you to understand that you are Field-Marshal Montgomery's personal representative on the bridge." He was the most delightful fellow, but got hopelessly tied up as to who was in command of who, writing masses of names down in his notebook, none of which can have conveyed anything to him. Still, he went away delighted with everything, ending up by telling us that he was wearing every stitch of clothing with which he had ever been issued, and I certainly have never seen anyone with so many clothes on.

In the evening, there was the most tremendous explosion in the town and I raced out of my headquarters, fearing the worst—the bridge had undoubtedly gone up. I conjured up thoughts of my being court-martialled. As far as I could see, blowing the bridge was just as grave an offence as not blowing the bridge, so that in a crisis one was bound to collect a court-martial whatever one did. At night it was so much on my mind that it played a major part in every dream I had. However, the bridge was not blown; a Sherman tank had fired its seventeen-pounder gun by mistake, blowing an American jeep to bits and unfortunately causing casualties.

Visitors kept coming to my headquarters all through the night and more alarmist reports reached us from various sources, but nothing material happened, although we had good reason to suppose that the enemy were not very far distant. It was, therefore, decided that in the morning the 3rd Royal Tank Regiment would go out complete and sit on the high ground on the far side of the river so as to be able to give anyone coming our way a hot reception. David Fyffe's machine-gun platoon went with them and took up a position in the little village of Boiselles. Still nothing appeared and as far as enemy activity was concerned the day was peaceful enough. But in Dinant itself we had more visitors than ever and we began to keep a visitor's book, the pages of which filled rapidly, with the names of people from every conceivable different type of unit. Fresh reports of enemy movement reached us and there now seemed to be no doubt whatever but that sooner or later the Germans were going to come up against us.

11 Platoon, having been relieved from their railway bridge, rejoined us and we prepared ourselves for what we thought might

be an extremely eventful night. The tanks remained in their forward positions, completely unprotected by infantry, and there was nothing to stop parties of German infantry from by-passing them and making an attempt to seize the bridge.

The American Air Service Corps and Captain Trotter's police were now becoming very dubious of their position the wrong side of the river, and it only needed one rather exciting incident to persuade them to pack up and cross the bridge to our side.

On the far bank was a road running alongside the river and at one point this road passed through a hole carved out of the rock, through which a Sherman tank could just squeeze. We had a post at this rock manned by Sergt. Baldwin's carrier section, whose function was to stop all personnel and vehicles and examine all papers. The sentries who were doing the checking had a Very light pistol which they were to fire if any vehicle would not stop. whereupon Sergt. Baldwin was to pull a string of mines across the road at the exit to the hole in the rock.

At about midnight up went a Very light and across were pulled the mines. A deafening explosion rent the night air and I again expected to see a yawning gap where the bridge once was, not having myself seen the light signal. A jeep which had refused to stop had been blown to bits and three very dead and shattered Germans lay in the roadway. They had been riding in a captured American jeep and were wearing American greatcoats over their German uniforms, in the pockets of which were found very detailed plans of our defence. The explosion had been so great that it unfortunately broke the jaw of an American standing some considerable distance away. This success buoyed us up no end, but the sight of the dead Germans was too much for Captain Trotter, who decided there and then that he was quite definitely on the wrong side of the river, so the morning of Christmas Eve arrived with the far bank completely clear of our American friends.

The advanced elements of the German 2nd Panzer Division were now a very short distance from Dinant and the tanks had spent a very uncomfortable night with enemy infantry patrols all round them. They managed nevertheless to get safely to their day positions a short while before the leading German tanks hove in sight from the neighbourhood of Foy-Notre-Dame. The great news came over the wireless that three Panthers and a "Mark IV" had been knocked out and hopes ran high.

At about the same time the machine-gun platoon, also moving out to its day positions, ran into some very unexpected trouble. A section trying to move down towards Foy-Notre-Dame was chased by a six-wheeled armoured car, which appeared from the village, so it beat a hasty retreat to Boisselles. The next thing that happened was that the whole platoon found itself cut off in Boisselles. However, some great work by the 3rd Royal Tank Regiment saved the situation and they managed to get back, but Boisselles had to be left in the hands of the enemy.

Things had certainly warmed up and Christmas Eve had the prospects of being an extremely exciting day. Then all activity suddenly died down. The Germans had taken a nasty and rather unexpected knock and this made them sit down and scratch their heads, before deciding what to do next. During the remainder of the day not a shot was fired by either side. What were the Germans going to do next? was the question we now asked ourselves. Documents which had been captured stressed the importance of fighting at night, and the popular theory was that they would try and come on again that night. It was now much too risky for the tanks to be out on their own during the hours of darkness, so it was decided that 11 and 12 Platoons would move out at last light to join them.

The refugee problem had by now become very serious and the roads were jammed with them as they had been in 1940. Enormous queues formed to cross the bridge and by the end of the day hardly a civilian was left in Dinant. The Germans' plans for creating alarm and despondency amongst the Belgians had achieved no small measure of success and the roads might soon have become almost impassable to military traffic. A pitiable sight it all was. Women and children, haggard and weary, were stumbling along carrying bundles of bedding and anything else they could manage, not knowing where they were going—just hoping to escape the battle and the Germans. For the second time in under five years this terrible tragedy had overcome these poor innocent people. What was worse, they knew the horrors of the first time and their faces now bore expressions of terror mingled with despair. Reports of German S.S. atrocities against the civilians came in from all sides and quickly spread amongst the fleeing columns. It was indeed sad to think that this Christmas of 1944, instead of being a time of Christian rejoicing, was bringing so much misery and distress to so many people, whose only desire was to live in peace and to carry on quietly with their daily tasks.

My headquarters had had more visitors than ever during the day, and various American gunner units arrived "out of the blue" and placed themselves under my command. Their general attitude was that they had to spend Christmas somewhere, so it might as well be at Dinant, and they were all as keen as mustard to have a crack at the Boche. I gladly accepted all these kind offers of help, as I foresaw that we might easily need every man upon whom we could lay hands. The crossing had to be held at all costs, and we took the precaution of laying in extra supplies of food and ammunition in case we should be cut off in our position. Everything was taken into consideration, even to the extent of issuing us with ten carrier pigeons which, when released, would fly back with messages to 21st Army Group at Brussels. They were lovely birds and with them arrived their rations and a pamphlet, couched in the best Army "Q" language on their maintenance. Their arrival provided us with a very welcome light interlude, and after much animated discussion a caretaker, in the person of the faithful and versatile Hodgson, was found. We were very tempted to dispatch one bearing Christmas greetings from us all to "Monty". Among the other offers of help I received was an appeal by the handful of American Air Service Corps personnel, left behind as a holding party for their billets, to be allowed to go out on patrol. I had tactfully and politely to refuse this request, as I did not want to add to the already large numbers of nondescript formations wandering about the countryside.

Darkness fell once more on this confused turmoil and we prepared ourselves for a disturbed night. Surely we would be attacked, even if it was only in patrol strength. There was an ominous quiet in the cold night air, which was not broken till shortly before midnight, when, without any warning, a few shells fell on the town. One of them fell not very far away from one of the American gun crews on the bank of the river. This was evidently too much for them, and their commanding officer arrived at my headquarters panting and said, "They've got me pin-pointed; I'm gonna move my position." We quietened the poor fellow down and he returned to his gun. Whether or not he moved it I don't know, but anyway nothing more fell near him and we did not see him again.

Just before this incident, orders had come through for us to turn from the defensive to the offensive on Christmas day, and plans were accordingly made for us to sally forth with the 3rd Royal Tank Regiment, in the morning. It was still highly possible, however, that the Germans would have a crack at us first, but at any rate the news was encouraging, as fresh divisions were arriving on the scene and the 29th Armoured Brigade was going to be no longer the lone guardian of the long stretch of river line it was then holding.

Christmas day, 1944, dawned and with it came the turning of the tide and the doom of what we hoped was the enemy's last desperate gamble—a gamble which, if it had come off, as at one time seemed possible, might have lengthened our careers as soldiers for many a long day.

Our first Christmas greetings from the Germans arrived in the form of a salvo of shells which fell at widely scattered points in the town; hardly a message of good-will on this festival day. Then the darkness lifted, revealing to our eyes the most beautiful morning—cloudless blue sky, not a breath of wind, white frost everywhere and the weak, watery sun climbing into the heavens. It was going to be a wonderful day for the air force and, as will be seen, they took every advantage of it.

At about eight o'clock two columns, each consisting of a squadron of the 3rd Royal Tank Regiment, a motor platoon and a section of carriers, set forth on parallel roads, one directed on Sorinne and the other on Boisselles. Here we were expected to meet up with the 2nd United States Armoured Division and would form right flank protection for them as they moved south. The remainder of the force were to remain in Dinant until such time as they were relieved by the 53rd Division and would then catch us up and rejoin us.

The advance to Sorinne was unopposed, but the column directed on Boiselles found the village to be held, and 12 Platoon, supported by the tanks, had to put in an attack to clear it. This attack was successful and a useful haul of prisoners was sent back. The column then consolidated in the village to await the arrival of the Americans.

Meanwhile, we had connected up with the reconnaissance regiment of the U.S. 2nd Armoured Division in Sorinne, and they told us that their tank battalions were about to put in an attack on a ridge of high ground overlooking the village of Foy-Notre-Dame, which as far as we knew was still held by the enemy. On this ridge was a farm which looked as if it might contain the enemy H.Q. It looked as if we were going to have a grandstand view of the battle, which was going to be all the more interesting as we had never seen an American armoured division in action before. So we found a convenient little plateau on the southern outskirts of Sorinne, where we settled down to await developments. It felt as though we were merely going to watch another of those demonstrations we had seen so many times before in England. Next day, however, we had the opportunity of surveying our grandstand from the enemy side, and were very shaken to see what a perfect machine-gun target we must have been.

At first all seemed peaceful on the objective and then figures of men in quite large numbers began running about. Some said they were Germans, some Americans, and the confusion was increased when two large tanks could be seen silhouetted against the sky-line. They looked very like Panthers and then someone said that they were American tank destroyers, which completely bewildered us. The Germans had been using a great deal of captured American equipment and these controversial steel monsters facing us could be one of three things—Panthers, tank destroyers manned by Americans, or tank destroyers manned by Germans.

However, we had not long to wait before we heard the distant throb of aircraft and, with engines screeching, a squadron of Lightnings roared over us and circled low over the opposing ridge. It evidently did not take them long to make up their minds that they were going to have a festive Christmas day, having reported back that the various objects about which we had been arguing were in fact three Panthers, a certain amount of German transport and a large number of entrenched infantry. This German force was subjected to merciless and incessant attack from the Lightnings, who soon began to dive to rooftop height with machine-guns blazing, dropping bombs at the same time, the explosion of which rocked our grandstand some thousand yards away.

It really was a wonderful spectacle, which gladdened our hearts and which compensated greatly for our Christmas day lunch of bully sandwiches and a mug of tea. I hope it will never be necessary to spend another Christmas day in these circumstances, but the morning of the 25th December, 1944, will live in my memory as one of the most satisfactory Christmas mornings I have ever experienced in my life.

After a short while, the Fm de Mahenne was reduced to rubble and all its outbuildings were either destroyed or blazing fiercely. Any German still left alive was well underground and no trace of movement came from the Americans' objective. It seemed quite impossible that any living thing could have survived the punishment of fire and brimstone meted out by the Lightnings. A space of a few minutes elapsed after the last wave of planes had disappeared from sight, and then from our left came a perfectly deployed formation of some fifty Sherman tanks of the 2nd Armoured Division. They were advancing very slowly, almost like a drill movement, towards the objective with their machine-guns blazing continuously. Thousands of rounds of ammunition must have been expended on that attack, which met with no opposition whatever, and it made one wonder how the American supply services could cope with the demands made upon them if this was an everyday occurrence. But one could not but admire the precision and thoroughness of the operation—no chances were taken and there was no doubt that if the ammunition was available, then this was the obvious course to take.

The American attack was entirely successful and we were able to watch them through our glasses collecting in large numbers of dazed prisoners. Next day too, we were able to go and see for ourselves the scene of the action and we found the area littered with German dead. The Panther tanks were almost untouched and quite usable, the crews having thought that it was safer under the ground than in their houses of steel.

While this battle was in progress, our mortars decided that they must have their share in the Christmas festivities too, and accordingly mixed in their quota of bombs with those of the Lightnings. On the grandstand with us all this time was the Colonel of the American reconnaissance regiment standing alongside his command jeep, which had the most enormous wireless aerials sticking out from everywhere. He was enjoying watching his own division as much as we were, but we could see he was itching to get on the go himself again. The ridge having been taken and consolidated, orders came over the air to him to move into and clear the little village of Foy-Notre-Dame which lay beneath us. His face lit up and he rushed to the nearest available microphone and shouted something into it, which we could not catch. However, we had not long to wait before three breathless American officers arrived on the scene and were told quite simply to get cracking and clear Foy-Notre-Dame. They asked no questions and requested no information as to what the form was. Off they dashed and a few minutes later a column of jeeps bristling with automatic weapons hurtled past us bound for the village. I am sure they never realized that there were still some two hundred Germans in Foy-Notre-Dame and they soon began to have casualties. However they did sterling work and rounded up numerous prisoners. The village, nevertheless, was nowhere near clear, when the wave of jeeps swept on to undertake bigger and better tasks which lay ahead of them. Those men of the reconnaissance regiment were great chaps and it really was grand to see their enthusiasm, dash and complete disregard of their own safety. The 2nd American Armoured Division had left a deep impression on us and a spirit of really close co-operation had existed between them and ourselves. Daylight was just beginning to fail, when we were ordered to complete the clearing of Foy-Notre-Dame and it looked as if it might be an unpleasant and difficult task in the failing light. 11 Platoon and a troop of tanks of the 3rd Royal Tank Regiment were selected to do the job.

The village was found to be full of German vehicles and equipment, including administrative vehicles which led us to believe that it must have been an advanced headquarters. 11 Platoon set about the job of searching every house and barn in the village and this long and laborious quest eventually yielded forty-two prisoners. One of these had to be fetched down from the top of the church steeple where he was hiding. On another occasion seven Germans were reported as being in a barn, the doors of which were bolted and locked, so collecting a stout and heavy ladder and using it as a battering ram, two riflemen charged the door, which immediately caved in. To their surprise seven very frightened Germans came out in single file with their hands clasped above their heads. Eventually this fantastic game of hide and seek came to an end and we were able to report Foy-Notre-Dame as clear of enemy.

And so Christmas night found us spread over a wide stretch of countryside. 12 Platoon remained in Boisselles, 11 Platoon in Foy-Notre-Dame, and the remainder of us at Sorinne. The sixth Christmas Day of war had come to an end—an unforgettable day, which had yielded most satisfactory results. The mass of captured German equipment as well as the prisoners had provided all with Christmas presents far better than we could have got in England, and all this had been achieved at the negligible cost of one slightly wounded man. The Colour-Sergeant arrived up with a bumper Christmas mail and most of us sat down —some lucky ones by fires, others less fortunate, outside in the freezing night—to read news of our families at home, which made us cast our minds back to former Christmas evenings by the fireside.

The night passed quite peacefully and at first light on Boxing Day we changed our dispositions slightly to fit in with the changing scene. 11 Platoon moved with their squadron of tanks on to the high ground—the scene of the previous day's battle. Here they were spasmodically shelled during the day, but, despite the hardness of the frozen ground, managed to dig down and so avoid serious harm. 10 Platoon moved off with another squadron to the neighbourhood of Celles, where they co-operated with and assisted the Americans in clearing woods of the remaining Germans, their only two casualties being caused by American machine-gun bullets. 12 Platoon remained based on Boisselles and sent out several local patrols. Nightfall found us in much the same position as the previous night with 11 Platoon back in Foy-Notre-Dame, reinforced by the Antitank Platoon and 10 Platoon back in Sorinne at the end of their day's work.

The general picture was becoming clearer at last. There was no doubt that the German spearhead had taken a very nasty knock and it now remained to be seen whether Rundstedt would try and pull out or whether he would come on again. In view of the forces still at his disposal, the latter course seemed the most likely. The stout-hearted American pockets still holding out at various strategic communication centres were giving him a big headache, which accounted for us finding large numbers of German vehicles of all kinds quite intact but without a drop of petrol in their tanks.

The next day was very peaceful, with us all remaining where we were. At last we were able to take stock and look around at the scenes of the actions of the last few hectic days. The village of Foy-Notre-Dame was well worth a visit. Its world-famous old church which stood right in the centre of this peaceful and picturesque little village, had miraculously escaped injury. All around it buildings had been burnt out or had had gaping holes torn in them by shell-fire. Yet not one pane of glass in the lovely church windows had even been cracked. The local priest was overwhelmed with gratitude and handed out souvenir folders containing pictures of the church and details of its history to everyone who came to see it.

By the following day the sound of battle had grown very distant and we were moved south to the little village of Mesnil Eglise, where we were to hold ourselves in readiness for any German counter-attack. The weather had turned even more arctic and our move was made very difficult by the frozen roads. Our route lay through Dinant, which was beginning to come to life once more—it was good to see the confidence of the local inhabitants returning, and we fervently hoped that they would never have to leave their houses again.

Mesnil Eglise was to be our home for the next nine days. This small, primitive and typically rural hamlet turned out to have a veritable heart of gold. The inhabitants had never seen Allied troops before and they extended to us the most wonderful welcome. The whole Company was billeted in cottages and cafes all over the village and everyone was very soon well and truly "dug in." On New

Year's Eve revelry went on all over the village till the early hours, which made up in some measure for our austerity Christmas.

Our military activities mainly consisted of reconnoitring positions in the event of counter-attack, and as we were fairly remote from the field of battle, we were able to relax considerably and make up some much-needed sleep.

The weather was still extremely cold and much snow fell, making the countryside look very lovely. On the other hand movement of vehicles became even more of a problem and, the village being down in a hollow, I wondered at times if we would ever manage to move out of it when the time came.

Although we were able to relax physically yet mentally we still had to be on the alert. A very amusing incident, which became widely known throughout the village as "le farce sur le Capitaine," illustrated the pitch of mental alertness to which we had become trained. One evening, as Kenneth Chabot and I were sitting writing letters and knocking back the odd drink, there was a knock at the door and the worried face of Sergt. Telford appeared. I went out to him, fearing something awful had happened, but was told I must not take the ensuing events seriously. Two members of 12 Platoon appeared, most skilfully dressed up—one in the guise of a woman. Kenneth was informed these had been picked up by the sentries and were suspected spies. I could scarcely restrain my laughter when they were taken into our room by an armed escort and Kenneth set about questioning them in a very businesslike manner. The so-called woman spy merely answered "nein" to all his questions and after a few minutes he rushed out of the room breathless with excitement and told me with bated breath that he could see by her figure that she was no "flicking" woman, and what was more, she spoke German. He next doubled the armed guard on the prisoners and sent for a truck to take them to Regimental Headquarters. At this point I had quietly to intervene. His leg had been well and truly stretched and the news spread round the village like wildfire. The local populace wherever we went in France and Belgium always took Kenneth to their hearts, and I am convinced that the magic name of the "Capitaine noir" will be remembered by many for years to come.

After many false starts and scares, we eventually bade farewell to Mesnil Eglise and moved some dozen miles farther east to another typical Ardenne village, Lavaux-St. Anne.

The weather was still extremely arctic and snow lay deep on the ground. The roads being icebound made the move a very tricky operation, especially for our carriers, which slid hopelessly about from one side of the road to the other.

By now, Rundstedt's Christmas offensive had been got well under control. He realised that he had shot his bolt and he now had to resort to trying to extricate as many of his Panzer divisions as he could from the closing net formed by the British and American armies. Surely, we thought, this was the Germans' last fling.

Our operational commitments not being very great, our main task was to keep ourselves warm and amused. Wild boar hunting provided us with a new form of sport. Most of us had not the faintest idea what a wild boar looked like and we were entirely ignorant of the method of hunting them. So we found an old hunter, who was thrilled with the idea of taking us out, and it was not long before the first expedition set out on its mission to find and destroy a wild boar. We looked an extremely odd collection tramping through the snow, armed with shot guns, sten guns, rifles and Bren guns. Certain of us were placed by the hunter in strategic positions on paths and rides in the woods while the remainder would try and drive a boar towards us. The whole procedure was very dangerous, as the beating consisted mainly of blazing off with Sten guns into the undergrowth, with very little regard for the safety of the guns waiting at the other end. A great deal of energy was expended by many of us during these hunts, which unfortunately proved to be fruitless. Only one wild boar was seen and it made off after James Ramsden had slightly wounded it. Still it was good exercise and produced many laughs, culminating in the great success achieved by our two lone hunters, Donald Sudlow and Eric Yetman.

These two decided, one afternoon, to go for a stroll through the woods, and after they had gone some way they spied a wild boar just in front of them. Both were armed with pistols and, drawing them, they fired at and badly wounded the animal, which retired into some nearby bushes. Realizing it might become dangerous, help was summoned and a rifle bullet administered the *coup de grâce*.

The local inhabitants said that this was the biggest wild boar they had seen for many years and it certainly looked the most ugly savage beast. Several of the organized shooting party went so far as to confess that they would never have taken part in the hunt had they seen this enormous beast in the first place.

After a few days at Lavaux-St.-Anne, it became evident that we were going to be pinched out of the battle-front, and hopes ran high that we would be able to return to Poperinghe.

An advance party, to our delight, was then called for, and set off for Menin, which was a quite acceptable substitute for Poperinghe. Our tank friends were also returning to that part of the world to resume once again the task of re-equipping themselves with the new tanks.

However, a few hours after the advance party had left, through came the shattering news that we were instead to return to the northern battle-front on the borders of Holland and Belgium. This was a bitter pill to take, but, as had happened so many times before, the first pangs of disappointment soon wore off and we resigned ourselves to what we thought would be our cold and very muddy fate.

And so our three and a half week stay in the Ardennes had come to an end. It had been a period packed full with excitement, amusement and interest, and although it completely wrecked our Christmas I don't think many of us would have missed it for the world. Our casualties over the whole period had been negligible, and in the few days in which we really saw action we had managed to achieve quite a measure of success. Whatever the future had in store for us, it was quite certain that the memory of Yuletide at Dinant would never fade. Riflemen, for many years to come, would at Christmastime, round their home fires, recount to their families the story of Christmas, 1944.

CHAPTER XI

INTERMISSION

ON the 14th of January we set off on a two-day trek to Bree. We did not know what we were going to be expected to do there, but we assumed that it was merely a stepping-stone to another long watch on the Maas. The place certainly did not look very inviting on the map.

The journey had the prospects of being, and in fact turned out to be, a veritable nightmare. The roads almost the entire way were coated with a thick layer of ice and the carriers had not a hope of making any headway. So a half-track had to be detailed to look after each carrier and tow it when necessary.

Our route lay through Namur to St. Trond, where we spent the first night, the whole Company being billeted in a convent school, where great kindness was shown to us by some English nuns, who ran the place. We had now passed from the beauty of the Ardennes to the flatter Belgian countryside, with which we had become so familiar.

All through the night, odd vehicles, which had dropped out of the column during the drive up, trickled in and next morning we set off again fairly complete. After passing through Hasselt, we moved on north to Hechtel and then swung east to Bree. The going was almost as bad as the previous day, except for the merciful fact that there were not so many hills, and everyone who had anything to do with the driving or guiding of the vehicles was very weary when the end of our journey hove in sight.

Bree, at first sight, looked no better than it did on the map. In addition, everything was very disorganized owing to the advance parties having had very little time to arrange accommodation before we arrived. However, by nightfall everyone was ensconced in private billets, and the general opinion was that we might have fared a great deal worse. Word went round that we would probably be here for two weeks, and this was a welcome contrast to our expectations of a return to the boring and uncomfortable existence on the banks of the Maas.

The next event of importance was to be our "ersatz" Christmas day, which was fixed for the 21st of January. It was going to be a white Christmas at any rate, and, even if the date was wrong, nothing was going to stop us having a really good day. The preceding few days were spent in cleaning up and sorting ourselves out, and the arrival of Christmas day found us all in the best of spirits.

Festivities began early and by lunch time everyone was in tremendous form. Our dining-hall was in a large café, which had been gaily decorated for the occasion. The tables had been beautifully laid out and a great variety of Christmas fare rested on top of the "Persil"-white tablecloths, loaned to us by the local Convent. Plates were piled high with food and the dinner, helped down by beer and Guinness, was voted as good as any we had had on previous Christmas days in the Army. Amidst all this rejoicing and hilarity, one solemn toast was drunk—to the memory of those who by their sacrifice had helped so much towards our success and who were not able to share with us the fruits of our victory to date. The names of many of our good friends, who had not been so fortunate as ourselves, passed through our minds at that moment—their sacrifice had not been in vain and they would live for ever in our memories.

After the Christmas dinner was over, all went off to their billets, some to continue the merry-making and others, with less strong constitutions, to sleep off the effects of the heavy meal.

We had taken the biggest café in Bree for a Company party in the evening. A dance band was in attendance, and a certain amount of dancing went on under very difficult conditions, due to lack of floor space. But everyone enjoyed themselves to the full and the party was an unqualified success. The Company's private funds were completely cleaned out, but it was well worth it, for we had little idea as to when we would next be able to celebrate in a big way. And so ended our "make believe" Christmas. We had tried our best to make it seem like the real thing, and I don't think we did too badly.

The following day, when many of us were not feeling at our best, was the one "Monty" had chosen to visit the Division for an investiture of the men who had won awards since D Day. This ceremony took place in a large public hall at Weert, and after it the Field-Marshal talked at some length to the crowded assembly. He was in great form and spoke with great optimism and conviction about the future. Much had still to be done, he told us, but it would be accomplished with the same precision and thoroughness as the decisive battles we had fought and won in 1944. He admitted that Rundstedt's Ardennes offensive had set back our plans, but he did not seem unduly worried by this.

After his talk, he was photographed with the recipients of the awards and then drove away, leaving behind an air of confidence amongst us all, instilled into us by his remarkable personality. There was no doubt that "Monty" had something which no one else had got.

The Christmas feeling had still not completely worn off when we heard that the Divisional Commander was coming to visit us the next day. General "Pip" Roberts' visits were always most delightfully informal, and this one was no exception to the rule. He walked round our area, stopping and talking to men he met on the way, and then asked me to show him a typical billet. Now this raised rather a difficult question. Everyone was so spread out that I was not absolutely sure which houses contained members of the Company and which did not. So after hasty consultation with the Sergeant-Major, I managed to keep the General talking for a few minutes while he rushed off to the office to check up on a suitable billet. The Company Clerk nobly volunteered that his room would be a good example, but on closer examination it turned out that his bed had not been made or the room tidied in any way whatever. The unfortunate woman with whom he was billeted was severely reprimanded and raced upstairs to set the room in order. This was done in record quick time, and the General was most impressed by it and asked me whether the whole Company lived in such luxury, to which I made a qualified reply. An awkward situation had been miraculously retrieved.

For the next three weeks we remained peacefully at Bree. On several occasions we nearly had to take our turn in the line, but were spared that discomfort each time at the last minute. Instead we were left undisturbed to have our biggest and best break since D Day. Many firm friendships were made with the townspeople which live to this day.

We had had many newcomers to the Company since we had last really been in action, and much time was devoted during these few weeks to training for the next phase of the campaign, which had the prospect of being extremely hard and bitter. We aimed to leave Bree one hundred per cent. ready as regards men and equipment, for what the future might bring, and I think we were not far short of that target.

However, in spite of all the training, we had plenty of time to enjoy ourselves and this we also accomplished with a fair measure of thoroughness. Home leave to England was going on all the time, even though many were disappointed at the slowness of the scheme. I think the Press had rather given many the false idea that the whole B.L.A. would be able to stream home regardless of military commitments, and the prospect of some of our Normandy members having to wait till April for their turn to go home came as rather an unpleasant shock.

Short leave to Brussels, however, was going strong, and there were by this time not many Riflemen who could not produce from their pockets a tattered piece of paper bearing some address in that gay city. Brussels leave had become such an integral part of our Army life that I have thought it worth while to include at this stage a Rifleman's impressions and reactions during such a trip. It is not meant to be a detailed description, but rather an attempt to show just what sort of things struck us and impressed us on our first visit in war-time to a European capital, where life, if it was not exactly normal, was in fact gay and novel.

"It was wet and it was cold, someone was making vague references to a brass monkey, but I smiled happily upon all and sundry; in fact I indulged in the old merry quip and jest as I splashed my way through the mud to the track taking me back to the Echelon. There is something about Dutch mud, especially the kind that lies around the banks of the Maas. It clings to you in a manner that is almost affectionate, it seems loath to let you go without giving you something of itself, and there seems to be so very much of it. But I digress; the reason for the light-hearted manner and the winning smile was that I was going to leave the war to take care of itself for a day or so, whilst I indulged in a little high life in Brussels, a city where life is something to be enjoyed rather than endured.

"How often during the past few weeks had I dreamed of this moment, when I could leave fear, mud and Guy's 'duff' behind me for a few days and step out into a world where pretty girls, hot baths, and clean crisp sheets were part of the natural order of things. Travelling back in the Echelon wagon, I was assailed by those self-same fears that had gripped me during the previous days in the field. Would I ever make it ? Would some stray missile or passing Jerry patrol put paid to my dreams of two days of luxurious living ? My fears were unfounded, and upon arriving at the Echelon harbour I was given the use—together with a dozen or so other chaps, two cows, an old sow and litter, and sundry chickens—of a nice comfy barn for the night.

"The following day I managed to scrounge some hot water and have a bath, borrowed as many francs (Belgian) as I could lay my hands on, and then, screwing up as much courage as I could, I asked for a new suit ! My request was received in deathly silence; I felt like the central figure in a pavement cartoon. The Quartermaster buried his face in his hands and rocked backwards and forwards in his chair, the tears trickling down between his fingers into his cup of 'char.' The Colour-Sergeant gave a short hysterical scream and flung himself from the room. Was this to be the fate of those beautiful suits that they had brought half-way across France ? It was cruel, cruel, like robbing a mother of her firstborn, but I refused to be influenced by tears, threats or the offer of a nice, partly-worn but slightly motheaten, relic. I stood adamant, and in the end had my way, whereupon I took my departure, bearing my prize aloft in triumph, and refusing the offers of innumerable guilders made by several shady-looking civilians standing in the roadway. The following morning, after making a final round of everyone who might conceivably be in possession of Belgian francs, we started off on the long journey to Brussels. I had not felt so excited since I was a small child waking up on Christmas morn.

"As we drew into Brussels I felt that it was really good to be alive. The mud, filth and horror of the battlefield lay far behind me. I felt that I had stepped straight into a modern, luxurious, pepped-up fairyland. There is a spring-like quality in the air of Brussels that seems to give one a terrific zest for living, and a desire to get rid of all one's worldly wealth in a very short space of time.

"British soldiery, who, in England, would complain bitterly at having to pay an extra halfpenny a pint for beer, go around distributing francs among the local populace in a manner that would do credit to a member of the Rothschild family.

"Brussels seems to be rather more Parisian in character than Paris itself. There are the same boulevardes—the Boulevard des Jardines Botaniques, for instance, that extremely wide thoroughfare famous for the Gare du Nord and the Café Blighty, and, of course, the very attractive female population. What is it that makes the girls of Paris and Brussels so attractive and exciting? Not mere beauty, but an indefinable and elusive something that is not to be found among the women of any other city in the world. I could expound at great length upon this fascinating subject, but I have always found discretion to be the better part of valour.

"Another remarkable thing about Brussels, apart from the young women, is the Black Market, Luxuries of all types can be had in plenty in this remarkable city; the only things that seem to be in short supply are the necessities. Champagne and silk stockings, and things of a like character, can be had for the asking plus, of course, a certain number of francs, while other things, without which the spark of life might flicker and go out, are conspicuous by their absence.

"Another thing that strikes the visitor (literally, if one is not quick on one's feet) are the Brussels trams. Brussels trams are spoken of with awe throughout the B.L.A. One does not travel *in* a tram—rather, one travels *on* it. If a seething mass of humanity is seen proceeding along the street at about ten miles an hour, you may be certain that, concealed by waving arms and legs and grinning faces, is a Brussels tram. It seems that the main object when a crowd boards a tram is to see that the driver's vision is completely hidden from view. The signal to move off is given. From time to time more people attach themselves to the backs of people who are already attached to the backs of those who are hanging on by tooth and nail. How to alight at the correct stopping place is, of course, the main problem, and it takes a considerable amount of practice before one is reasonably certain of getting off the vehicle within half a mile of the required destination. In fact, a journey by tram can be compared with some justice, to a journey into action in a fighting vehicle. I think, perhaps, that there may be just a shade more room on the fighting vehicle, which may explain why most of the men stationed in Brussels are only too anxious to leave the pleasures of this delightful city for rather sterner duties elsewhere.

"This desire 'to get up and at 'em' was pointed out to me by various members of the Brussels garrison at different times during my short stay. They assured me, with the tears practically streaming down their cheeks, that time and time again had they applied for permission to 'get up there' with the infantry and the tanks. But it was not to be. Not for them the fun and frolics of the front line. All that they could look forward to was the hard work and daily grind, the filling up of form after form. My heart bled for them as I shook them sympathetically by the hand. I know how they felt, the same way myself, only in the reverse order. Such is life.

"Another remarkable thing about Brussels is that the proprietors of the cafés, unlike their counterparts in London, actually look pleased to see you and do their best to see that you have a good time. Anything from beer (?) to champagne can be supplied, and there is usually a band and cabaret. The bands usually perform with great vigour, as also, incidentally, do the dancers. The natives of Brussels put their whole heart and soul into their dancing and proceed round the floor at a prodigious rate, waving their arms up and down all the while, somewhat in the manner of an over-worked pump-handle. I would rather not say anything about the cabaret shows—it would be kinder. The bands, but not the cabarets, differ in quality from one café to another, but they have one thing in common. They each play 'Tipperary' (which they regard as the British National Anthem) at least two dozen times during an evening, mixed up with the latest German song hits. At the end of my visit I felt that if anyone played 'Tipperary' again, I would destroy them by tearing them limb from limb. Of course, there are cafés where the hospitality is of an even more generous nature, but I won't go into that now.

"Like every other large town throughout the world, there are various large buildings of one kind and another, which according to the guide book, 'simply must be seen.' In my opinion, buildings in one town are very similar to those in any other: it is only the people that differ. I think that very few soldiers spend much of their time in examining different specimens of architecture during their brief forty-eight hours leave.

"Which brings me to another point. According to some newspaper correspondents, British soldiers wanted nothing so much as to get in with some Belgian family during their stay, and to wheel the baby about in a pram. I know that newspaper correspondents don't always get their stories quite right, but I have always regarded this fantastic tale as their best and brightest effort. Show me the man who wanted nothing, only to wheel a baby about in a pram, while all the delights and pleasures (practically) of the Arabian Nights lay before him, and I will show you the most remarkable man yet to be admitted into this remarkable Army. Any man who can resist the atmosphere of perpetual spring that surrounds Brussels is no man, but a graven image.

"Of course, time, as I believe someone has already pointed out, waits for no man. So some forty-eight hours after our arrival in Brussels found us on our way back to the slit trenches and the everlasting 'brew.' At the start of the journey we discussed, somewhat hopefully, the chances of breaking down before we had proceeded very far. But as we progressed talk gradually ceased. We just lay back dreaming of all that had taken place during the previous two days.

"So it was that we arrived back at the Company. The usual jests were made and hotly denied. The presents we had bought were inspected by the critical, if somewhat envious, eyes of our friends, and we were told that we should be on guard in half an hour.

"So we slipped back into the old life once more, with just one difference; during our periods of 'stag' we could always cast our minds back and live once again those magical forty-eight hours.

"Before ending this short chapter, I would like to say that the Belgian people will always be held in high esteem by the men of the British Army. I except one man only from the above; and he was the man who rewarded two friends and myself with a cigar each, after we had extinguished a small fire in his car. It was a mean thing to do to three unsuspecting soldiers. After smoking half an inch of the cigars, we wished we had let his car burn out!

"In conclusion, one cannot stress too much the importance of this brief interlude in the grim life we were living. Spending two days among friendly people in a large city with an almost peace-time atmosphere brought a breath of sanity back to our battle-shocked minds."

Towards the end of January, plans were made for us to move back to Flanders to the town of Roulers and in fact our indefatiguable advance party actually went there and began organizing things for us. But once again we were to be disappointed at the last moment. Infantry were still in too short supply.

Our eventual departure from Bree on the 11th of February came as a complete surprise. We were to leave the 11th Armoured Division and were to move north to the stretch of the Maas between Roermond and Venlo in Holland. Here we were to come under command of our old friends the 6th Airborne Division and help them out with their task of holding the river line.

We moved to the village of Helden, some three miles from the river, and took up our position as reserve battalion of the 5th Parachute Brigade. We were to be here for five days and then move up into the line to relieve another battalion. During this period we put in some practice at boating as it was thought possible we might have to send a patrol across the river. The remainder of the time was spent in some more limited training and cleaning up.

On the 15th of February, I took with me the platoon commanders on a detailed reconnaissance of the river line positions we were to take up the next day. Movement in vehicles was impossible due to the open nature of the country affording excellent observation to the enemy and we walked many miles that afternoon. On arrival back we were painfully surprised to hear that all our efforts had been in vain and that instead of taking up our prearranged position, we were in contrast going the opposite direction to Roosendaal, where we would return to the command of our parent division. We searched for Roosendaal on our maps. It looked fairly reasonable and was in the only part of liberated Holland we had not yet visited.

So once again our long column of vehicles set forth. Our route lay through Weert, Eindhoven, Tilburg, and Breda and the journey was neither interesting nor eventful.

Although our advance party had had very little time, they had done great work and when we arrived at Roosendaal, we found ourselves in some of the best billets we had ever had.

We still had absolutely no indication as to what we were going to do in the future and so once again we settled down to a period of training and emptied our vehicles of all stores. The Black Market was very evident in this town and crowds of people hung around our transport all day in the hopes of being able to buy something from us. Every single thing we had seemed to be in demand. The crowning incident occurred when one day Kingsmill emerged from the stores carrying in his hand a cake of blanco and an enthusiastic black marketeer rushed up to him, relieved him of the blanco, and pressed five guilders into his hand. What his reactions were on arriving home and opening his package we never discovered, but the blanco boom did not last long and no further deals were reported. However a brave bid had been made to introduce this new commodity to the Black Market.

The only signs of enemy activity in this part of Holland were the large number of flying bombs, which passed over us on their way to Antwerp. A terrific barrage from anti-aircraft guns used to greet them and a remarkably high proportion of them were shot down before reaching their ultimate destination. The natural reaction of us all was to rush into the streets and watch the shooting gallery, but we had to restrain ourselves owing to the danger of the falling fragments of the anti-aircraft shells.

Five peaceful days passed by with still no news of our future and then as usual orders came through without any previous warning. Again we were to leave the 11th Armoured Division, this time to join the 49th Infantry Division and assist them in holding a stretch of the Waal West of Nijmegen.

Our own division were coming under command of the First Canadian Army and were going to take part in the operation of rolling up the Siegfried Line from the north. As our armoured regiments had not yet completed the changeover to the new tanks the 4th Armoured Brigade was brought into the division. Included in this Brigade was a motor battalion of the "60th," which made us surplus.

The fighting in this battle between the Maas and the Rhine turned out to be some of the most unpleasant and bitterest of the campaign and our new task was an absolute luxury, compared to what we would have gone through, had we participated in that operation. So we could consider ourselves as being extremely lucky for a change.

The journey to the Waal was carried out by easy stages. Highways in this part of Holland were few and far between and a vast amount of traffic was on the move in preparation for the forthcoming battle. As a result we had very low priority and our road movement had to be carefully fitted in so as not to interfere with more important convoys.

The night of the 23rd of February found us at Tilburg. Here we spent the night in a monastery and our classical scholar, James Ramsden, was reported to have sat up all night talking to the Monks in Latin.

Next day we harboured just short of our destination in the little marshland village of Maasbommel, after a long and uninteresting drive.

The take over of the position from a squadron of the Manitoba Dragoons, the armoured car regiment of the Canadian Armoured Division, was scheduled to take place early on the morning of the 25th of February and everything went off without a hitch.

The little village of Dreumel, where we now found ourselves, was a very pleasant spot and quite an oasis in this land of eternal bog and swamp. Despite the fact that it was right in the front line, except for the usual shattered church spire, it bore few of the scars of war, which was surprising as the neighbouring village of Wamel was very badly shattered. Nothing much was known of the enemy facing us on the far bank of the river, but it was thought that they consisted largely of Dutch S.S. On our own side I had two platoons of Dutchmen under my command, who were apt to be rather a liability at times owing to their craze for blazing off with their weapons at the most unsuitable times. Still they meant well and although I think that their N.A.A.F.I. rations of cigarettes and chocolate were their main inspiration, they did some good work, and bolstered up our manpower situation.

Our "watch on the Waal" lasted for just over a fortnight and during this time nothing very sensational happened. The enemy used to send over occasional shells and mortar bombs and in the evenings they would have fits of "spandau" firing, but the only casualty during the whole of this period was suffered by a civilian. Our Bren gunners, snipers, mortars and attached machine-guns all fired a great number of rounds and even if they did not inflict many casualties on the enemy, it gave them a lot of valuable practice and experience under very peaceful conditions. A more domestic side of our life consisted of supervising Dutch civilians in the maintenance and repair of roads, if they could be called such.

At one time it was thought possible that we might have to do a raid across the river, and we put in a certain amount of boating practice, but the plan never materialized.

Survivors of the First Airborne Division from Arnhem were still making their way back to our lines and we kept a very close watch on the opposite bank of the river at night for any signals which might indicate to us that one of them wished to be collected and brought across.

On three occasions the agreed upon signal was spotted, but it was then thought that the enemy had found out the secret of the signal and were using it as a ruse against us.

James Ramsden took over command for six days, while I went away to Poperinghe to stay with the 3 R.T.R. The object of this visit was to give me an opportunity to see the new tanks and learn their capabilities. In addition we tried to refresh our memories of co-operation between an armoured regiment and a motor company in preparation for what we hoped would be the final battles in Germany. I was very impressed with the accuracy of the gun on the Comet, and was able to give encouraging reports to the Company when I returned. It was a time usefully as well as enjoyably spent.

The news from the northern battlefront had been most gratifying. After the long and bitter struggle undertaken by the 1st Canadian Army, the Americans had attacked across the River Roer from the south and in a remarkably short time had cleared the territory between the Maas and the Rhine of enemy and had linked up with the British and Canadians. The stage seemed now set for the crossing of the Rhine and the entry into Germany proper. Much preparation had to be made, but it looked as though the sooner we got across the easier it would be.

We decided to make our last night at Dreumel a gala one. As many Brens as we could muster poured a stream of tracer bullets across the river and our mortars, firing phosphorus smoke bombs, started some first-class fires amongst buildings, which we hoped contained enemy, Morale was very high when, on the morning of the 12th March, the Manitoba Dragoons returned to relieve us and we set out for Belgium once again.

The whole of the 11th Armoured Division was concentrated in the area of Diest and Louvain, prior to what we hoped would be the last battle of the war—the over-running of Hitler's stronghold.

It was to be a period of rest, preparation and recreation and we set out to make the most of it.

After another long, tiring and uninteresting drive by way of Eindhoven and Gheel, we arrived late in the evening at the village of Blauwberg, not many miles from Diest. The 29th Armoured Brigade were laid out in their Regimental Groups and we once again entered into partnership with the 3rd Royal Tank Regiment who were situated a few miles away from us in Aerschot.

Blauwberg was unsatisfactory for us in many ways and two days later we moved a couple of miles on to Hersselt. Here also things were not to our liking and once again we packed up and moved a few miles to the village of Ramsel.

At last we seemed to have found an ideal spot and we were all very happy with the prospect of a few weeks here. Our billets were good, the villagers were very friendly and altogether Ramsel was quite a gay little place.

But no ! This time we had unwittingly strayed into an area allotted to another formation and it was not long before we were pestered and attacked by officious town majors, telling us we must move. For four days we stood our ground and repulsed all efforts to evict us, but the odds were overwhelmingly against us and on the 20th March "Gulliver's travels" began all over again.

At last we came to rest permanently in Gelrode, a small village just outside Aerschot. This was a very pleasant and peaceful spot, where we were to spend a delightful week of warm and sunny spring weather.

Our only military activity consisted of each platoon doing a small scheme with their respective squadrons of the 3rd Royal Tank Regiment, and so refreshing their memories of former tactics as well as getting some idea of the capabilities of the new Comet tanks.

Our recreational activities consisted mainly of short leave as well as day trips to Brussels and nightly visits to Diest and Louvain. A good time was had by all and as we had constantly drilled into us, what to do and what not to do, with the emphasis on the not, in Germany, this period was popularly known as "The last Frat."

The 24th of March, a day we had all been eagerly awaiting, arrived. Another gloriously sunny and cloudless day. It was "D Day No. 2." Soon the sky was filled with the drone of aeroplane engines and looking up we saw countless streams of planes towing behind them gliders, containing our old and gallant friends, the 6th Airborne Division. It seemed an incredibly short time ago that we had been with them on the bank of the Maas and now they were on their way to drop on the far side of the River Rhine.

The tempo was certainly being kept up, which was very cheering and the Germans were surely going to find it hard to meet this new onslaught so soon after the resounding defeat they had suffered between the two big rivers.

That morning we heard the "Big Plan." The 51st Highland and 15th Scottish Divisions had made the assault crossing and through them were going the Guards Armoured and the 7th Armoured Divisions respectively. The 11th Armoured Division was in Army

Reserve and was going to be pushed through at the first suitable point where resistance showed signs of crumbling.

This had the prospects of being a great role and once we got through the first crust, we felt sure that nothing would stop us from "cracking about the plains of Northern Germany," to use Monty's own words.

Eagerly and with tremendous confidence, we awaited the signal to move forward. Memories of the trip from Laigle to Antwerp came back to our minds. Could it possibly be another "Swan"?

We had not long to wait.

CHAPTER XII

OVER THE RHINE

ON the 27th of March orders came through that we were to move up to the battle next day. The operation seemed to be going very much according to plan. Resistance was still stiff on the 30 Corps front in the north, but the going was much better on the 12 Corps sector. So it looked to us a fairly good bet that we would be pushed through somewhere south of 30 Corps and north of the 9th U.S. Army, who had made a bridgehead on the right flank of 12 Corps.

We were all very keyed up and the day was spent in loading and checking every detail to ensure that we were one hundred per cent. prepared to play our part in our greatest and what we hoped would be our final adventure.

At half-past five next morning, our long column of vehicles began wending their way down the village street of Gelrode. Our destination was still not settled, but we imagined that we would probably concentrate for the night somewhere north-east of Venlo between the Maas and the Rhine—a trip of about a hundred miles.

Our route lay through Diest and Beeringen and we cast our minds back six months to the time when we were advancing along this same road under less pleasant conditions.

On to Bree, and here the local population turned out to give us a great send-off. Familiar faces appeared from houses, cafés and shops everywhere and presents and wishes of good luck were showered on us. The people of Bree, I learnt afterwards, followed our progress during the next few weeks with the greatest of interest and anxiety. We appeared to have left a deep and lasting impression on them.

Striking east, we reached the banks of the Maas and followed the course of the river to Venlo. We had bade farewell to Belgium for the last time and once again were in Holland. The drive along the river was interesting to us, because it was the first time we had had the chance of seeing the Maas under safe conditions. Previously our only opportunity of studying these reaches of the river had been from camouflaged observation posts or by inviting a German sniper on the far bank to practise his skill.

Venlo, where we crossed, was very badly scarred by the marks of war. It had been under shell-fire during the entire winter and very few of its buildings had been untouched.

Now we imagined ourselves to be in the heart of the Siegfried Line and we scanned the countryside for immense fortifications, but beyond a fair sprinkling of trenches and sundry earthworks, nothing was visible to convince us of the truth of the stories we had heard of impregnable defences and anti-tank obstacles.

It was with keen excitement that we crossed the frontier into Germany. The frontier in itself was not thrilling—just the normal Customs huts, which by now we knew so well. I think our main urge was to see a German in his own country and we soon began studying the faces of small numbers of dejected-looking German peasants, trudging along the road or working in the fields bordering it. Once our first curiosity had been satisfied, they had no further interest for us.

Signs of war were not very evident until we reached Goch. Here the fighting had been very heavy and the town was a mere shell of its former self. Our minds went back to Normandy. And as we pushed on and reached Wesel the memory of those early days of the campaign came back to us even more clearly. The stench of dead cattle, the sickly smell of cordite, the shattered buildings and the chaos brought about by utter destruction—they were all there. Was this going to be the same the whole way across Germany? we kept asking ourselves. Wesel looked like Caen all over again—in fact it had been more completely destroyed than the Normandy town. Enormous modern buildings had just collapsed like packs of playing cards and not a sign of civilian life was evident anywhere.

The actual crossing of the Rhine was a great thrill. Unending columns of every description were queueing up to take their turn on the pontoon bridges, which were ringed by scores of anti-aircraft guns. In addition overhead cover, was provided by barrage balloons and by the vigilant patrol of Royal Air Force fighters.

It appeared that the battle must be going well as, contrary to our earlier expectations, we had now crossed the Rhine and were going to concentrate to the east of it. The fighting, however, could not have passed on long since as numerous dead bodies, nearly all German, lay unburied alongside the roads and in the ditches.

We halted for the night, just short of the village of Brunen in some open fields and, not quite knowing what the position was ahead, we took no chances and dug holes for ourselves. Congestion on the roads was very great and we seemed to be well and truly mixed up with the 7th Armoured Division. Brunen itself was a shambles and an appalling bottleneck for traffic.

During the day, we had covered nearly one hundred and forty miles and not one of our vehicles had broken down—a most gratifying performance, and we hoped that it augured well for the future.

The night passed without incident, and the next morning we teamed up with the 3rd Royal Tank Regiment, prior to an expected move about lunch-time. Information was still scarce, but it appeared that things were easing considerably on our front and the prospects of another Normandy slogging match were replaced by optimistic hopes of some steady "swanning."

Soon after lunch came the order to move and we set off down some tortuous tracks, where the going was extremely boggy. Many vehicles stuck but were all eventually pulled out, and on we all went, finally striking the road again at Raesfeld. Already we had gone farther than we had anticipated and I had been unable to give out any further orders to my platoon commanders. So it resolved into a question of following the vehicle in front and hoping for the best. For approximately fifteen miles we went on like this and eventually arrived at the little town of Velen. Not a sign of any hostile German had been seen the whole way and supreme confidence was the keynote again. Surely, however, it was not possible that we had already broken through the last crust of German resistance.

Velen was full of civilians and this was to be our first chance of dealing with them in the correct manner. They were all ordered to stay in their houses and we took over the buildings we needed for our own use, making the occupants evacuate and double up with their neighbours. An hour's notice we considered sufficient for this purpose, and there was never any reluctance on the part of the occupants to move out in this time.

The headquarters of the 3rd Royal Tank Regiment were in the local hotel, where the proprietor and his wife, within a short time of our arrival, produced plates of bacon and eggs. We did not quite know whether we should accept them or not, but to ease our consciences we produced in return the required amount of money which we had been told we would pay for eggs in Germany. Otherwise there was no question of fraternising on anyone's part and any friendly gestures by the German civilians were met by frigid British stares. After another quiet night, the following day, the 30th of March, we set off early in the morning with orders to crack on for all we were worth.

Our first check came at Holtwick, where a bazooka was fired at the leading tank. 10 Platoon dismounted from their half-tracks and, supported by the tanks and the leading section of carriers, began to advance on foot into the village. Very little opposition was met and we had soon cleared a way through and were ready to press on again. This was probably our first encounter with the German Home Guard. Their fighting ability was not very great and it did not need much persuasion to make them decide that an undamaged village was better than one reduced to ruins by shelling. The most intriguing part of their defence was in the shape of the inevitable road-block, which consisted of an enormous wooden drum, filled with sand, which was rolled across the road. We normally arrived too suddenly on the scene, however, for the rolling of the drum to be accomplished.

The advance continued through the villages of Asbeck and Schoppingen to the small town of Horstmar. Resistance all along the way was very slight and consisted mainly of small parties of surprised and completely unprepared enemy, together with the local Home Guard element in the villages.

The civilians everywhere appeared glad to see us and relieved that the war had passed by them. Many of them waved and threw fruit to us, but the non-fraternisation orders were still deep set in our minds and no one wavered.

It had been a great day. We had advanced some twenty-eight miles, had knocked out a great deal of enemy transport and had captured many prisoners and much booty.

The Royal Air Force were having great difficulty in keeping up with the fast-moving scene, and several times during the day we had to resort to one of our best friends—yellow smoke—when overhead planes displayed some measure of doubt as to our identity. During the afternoon a Typhoon made a crash landing amongst us and our stretcher-bearers evacuated the wounded pilot.

Horstmar was to be the limit of our advance for the day, and we settled down to make ourselves comfortable for what we hoped would be an uneventful night. Again we requisitioned houses and again the Germans obeyed our orders with the greatest alacrity. It all seemed too easy so far, and I feared that over-confidence would creep in again. From this point of view, it was possibly a good thing that we were in for a very busy night.

Carrier patrols had to be sent out to protect the Royal Engineers during a reconnaissance of a damaged bridge, and then again while they were repairing it. Finally, when it had been repaired, 12 Platoon had to go out and take up a position round it in all-round defence.

It was 11 Platoon however, who had the gayest and most exciting time. To our north lay the fair-sized town of Burgstein Furt, and the King's Shropshire Light Infantry had been ordered to move up and put in a night attack against it. In the dark they were very vulnerable in their vehicles and so we were told to produce a screen to cover their debussing, prior to the attack, the object of this being to enable them to reach a point as close as possible to their objective.

I ordered 11 Platoon to get into a position just south of Burgstein Furt astride the main road. They encountered no trouble in reaching their objective and based themselves on two houses either side of the road.

Very soon after their arrival, however, the fun began. German vehicles began "swanning" down the road, the occupants having no idea of the present military situation, and were either shot up or captured. A large collection of prisoners was assembled and bundled into the cellars of the houses, one German Colonel protesting volubly against being sandwiched in with other ranks.

The crowning incident, however, was the approach of two German Volksturm soldiers from the direction of Burgstein Furt, singing merrily and in apparently very good form. They had evidently had a good party in the town and were now returning to their homes. The shock of finding their houses occupied by British soldiers was too much for them and they were quickly bundled into their own cellars along with the rest.

The debussing of the K.S.L.I. passed without incident, and shortly afterwards, I was given permission to withdraw 11 Platoon back to us at Horstmar. They were in great heart.

The following morning, we parted company from the 3rd Royal Tanks and joined up again with the 23rd Hussars.

While this reshuffling was going on, yet one more laugh was added to our already good collection. 12 Platoon sent back a request over the air to be relieved of a small number of prisoners they had taken in their area. I accordingly dispatched Smythson in his jeep to collect them. The platoon position was a considerable way away up a road bordered by woods each side, which might have contained odd bodies of enemy for all we knew. The jeep, however, arrived safely at its destination and the prisoners were piled into and on to it. On the return journey, Smythson turned to have a word with the escort, but found to his horror that he had been left behind, and that he, in fact, was alone with six Germans. Displaying great coolness, however, he drove gaily down the road, slowing down at intervals to wave and shout to imaginary friends of his in the woods both sides. Proudly he handed over the prisoners at the end of his journey, providing us with the best laugh we had had for a long time.

The 3rd Tanks had in the meanwhile pushed on in company with the K.S.L.I., and immediately we had joined up with the 23rd Hussars we followed on after them, passing through the town of Emsdetten and crossing the River Ems just beyond. Eventually we came to rest in a field near the village of Sinningen. Again we had made an advance of close on thirty miles and had suffered no serious check. Once, however, we were strafed by a Focke Wulf 190 while resting in a field, but beyond causing some of us to cast our dinners into the mud as we flung ourselves to the ground, no inconvenience was caused. The incident, nevertheless, served as a timely reminder that the Luftwaffe still had some planes left and that it was now operating from its home bases. Air sentries were in great demand again.

We were now very close to the Dortmund-Ems canal, against which so many attacks had been launched by the R.A.F. It was a fair-sized water obstacle with wooded high ground on the far bank. It seemed ideal for defence, and if the Germans were not completely finished it seemed likely that they might make a stand here. It was now 1st of April, and we spent the greater part of the day resting in a wood, where we would not be seen by prying German aircraft.

Just as we were rejoicing at the thought of a good night's rest, however, orders suddenly came through that we were to make a bridgehead over the canal to enable the sappers to throw a bridge across it. Very little information was forthcoming about the enemy situation and so it was with a certain amount of caution that we motored to the banks of the canal. The sappers had received orders from a different source, which did not tally with ours, and it was accordingly with a certain amount of shame that we found that they had arrived before us. Their commander was very relieved to see us, however, as he had realized that his bridging apparatus was forming the spearhead of the advance.

No opposition was encountered in making the bridgehead and we were soon in position, surrounding the sappers, who quickly started work on the bridge. The canal had very little water in it, and we were thus able to see for ourselves the effect of the R.A.F.'s draining operations.

The night was quiet, except for the occasional drone of an evening reconnaissance plane, but we remained very alert and on the lookout for signs of a counter-attack.

We held our bridgehead till lunch-time the following day, and during the morning we collected in several prisoners from the neighbouring woods and killed seven out of ten of a German patrol which was taking an interest in our activities. This last encounter was most cheering and successful, giving us great satisfaction.

The bridge building had not proceeded as quickly as had been hoped, due to various difficulties, and we were therefore relieved by the 75th Anti-Tank Regiment to enable us to rejoin our Regimental Group, which had been ordered to cross the canal by a bridge which had been constructed farther north at Riesenbeck, where there had been heavy fighting by other units of the Division.

Motoring through burning villages, we eventually passed through the leading groups and arrived at the approaches to the town of Tecklenburg. Here fairly stiff opposition was met, and the other companies spent the rest of the day dealing with it. While this was going on, we were being spasmodically shelled on the road and were sniped at from the neighbouring woods. We had very few casualties, however, and managed to take quite a few prisoners. Many hundreds of rounds had been expended, too, in firing at enemy aircraft which tried ineffectively to bother us.

Darkness fell and we found ourselves in some very muddy fields outside Tecklenburg, with the unpleasant prospect of a night advance ahead of us.

Opposition was showing signs of stiffening all the way along and we seemed to have run into a more fanatical type of German soldier. Our ideas of an easy passage ahead faded into the background and we prepared ourselves for some hard fighting to come.

Nevertheless, in the background of our minds, we felt that victory could not be far off.

CHAPTER XIII

TO THE BANKS OF THE ELBE

READING the English newspapers at that time, one would have thought that fighting had virtually ceased and that all we were doing was to motor along and take thousands of prisoners. This annoyed us to no small degree and, as will be shown later in this chapter, two of our bitterest engagements were yet to be fought. Although undoubtedly things were going very well, yet valuable lives were still being lost daily, and we wished that some of these war correspondents who were sending back these totally inaccurate reports could be up with us to see what was really going on.

At 3 o'clock in the morning of 3rd of April, we extricated ourselves from the mud in which we had spent the last few hours and moved forward through the darkness, with the intention of seizing intact a bridge across the canal north-west of Osnabruck. Progress was very slow and various people got lost, which did not help matters. However, by first light the 3rd Tanks reported that they had an intact bridge at Everschede, which was good news.

The advance went on slowly and we began meeting scattered resistance. At midday, however, orders came through that we were to switch to the 3rd Tanks centre line, go through them and crack on as fast as we could with the object of getting an intact bridge over the canal near Bohnte—the last water barrier before the Weser. We decided that, in view of the very scattered and disorganized opposition, our best chances of success lay in going at full speed ahead and hoping that the bazookas would miss.

The only opposition at first was a certain amount of sniping, which caused a few casualties, but nothing serious was encountered until on turning east the two leading tanks were hit by an "88" and our column began to be shelled.

This put a check on the advance and the motor platoons, having dismounted, had to spend the rest of the day clearing the woods in the neighbourhood. They met no opposition however, and we could only suppose that the trouble had been caused by several German self-propelled guns, which had made off after their initial shelling of us.

While all this was going on the "F" Company group motored through us and secured the bridge without further opposition. Eventually we followed on behind them and got into our position holding the north of the bridgehead just after midnight.

Here we remained till light came, when the 3rd Tanks went through us again to take the lead, and for almost the remainder of the day we followed slowly on through Bohnte and Rahden, nothing of interest happening.

The 3rd Tanks had met a certain amount of opposition, however, and the end of the day found us again in the lead. Quite good progress was made, and when darkness fell we pulled up for the night at the village of Nordel.

Stolzenau was reached without much trouble in the early afternoon on 5th April, and this time we found a blown bridge. Perhaps the Germans were going to make a stand on the Weser. At any rate, we were going to be held up for a considerable time while a new bridge was constructed.

"G" and "H" Companies were ordered to make a bridgehead, and "H" Company was to cross first. The crossing was to be done in assault boats and in consequence no vehicles or heavy equipment could be taken over. The ground sloped down to the town of Stoltzenau in the direction whence we had come, but a steepish bank some twenty feet high, hid the river from the "home" side. Whilst "H" Company made their crossing south of the bridge under persistent fire from 88 mm. and 20 mm. airbursts, we lay low in the doubtful shelter behind the bank, receiving many of the overshoots.

It seemed that we lay behind that bank for a century, while we received our final briefing, checked our portable radio sets, and waited, waited, waited. A few 88 mm. H.Es. burst in the fields behind us to relieve the monotony of the airbursts overhead. The Colonel arrived, and gave us some words of encouragement, which were much appreciated. Years passed. We knew "H" Company were having a tough time and that did not help. Finally an order was received that "G" Company would cross on the northern side of the bridge, owing to the state of the opposition on our immediate front, and we made preparation to move. A high piece of ground separated our present position from the one selected as our new crossing place, and in order that we should not be observed crossing such an obvious hump, it was necessary to make a detour through some marshy undergrowth about a hundred yards back. As we made our way through the bushes crouching low, aerial rods, rifles, spades and all "the panoply of war" became entangled in the masses of briar and thorn, which, coupled with the fact that the ground was both sloping and slippery, made progress slow and awkward. We had no material cover between us and the enemy and it was necessary to rely on the camouflage of the foliage and providence. This finally accomplished without incident, we took cover behind a warehouse that backed down to the river. No sooner had we gained this position than a hail of 20 mm. tracer swept down over the marshy ground at waist level from which we had just emerged. We had been spotted—too late.

We had another wait here while the final preparations were made for the crossing, during which shelling by airburst persisted, punctuating the Spandau fire which, directed at "H" Company still establishing themselves, chattered away with regularity. The atmosphere was tense—as tense as it always was during those minutes of waiting before action. At last we received the command to make our way down to the riverside, a platoon at a time. We emerged from our cover of the warehouse, and turned right down what must have been the main street. After a fifty yards sprint, the river was swirling, black and menacing, at our feet. It was a good spot to cross "as good spots went," for we were completely out of sight of the enemy who were holding positions some hundreds of yards back across the water, owing to a ridge on the far side similar to the one on our own.

The Weser was wide and flowing fast—too fast to be pleasant. We knew that unless we could gain the opposite bank before the current had carried us too far down, the game was well and truly up, for the bridgehead was only a hundred or so yards in width. The bridge itself, was on our immediate right, and lay sprawled across the water, making the river swirl and eddy as it washed its way through the twisted girders. There were with us an R.E. Officer and some Sappers, already making plans for the building of a new bridge. The assault boats, flimsy craft of wood and canvas, lay to our left in a small inlet. There were not many of them, and it was apparent that a ferry service would be necessary to transport all of us across. 12 Platoon went over first, one of their boats being carried well down the river by the strong current before finally touching down on the other bank. 10 Platoon followed, with elements of 9, then 11, and Company H.Q. brought up the rear. The whole Company was across, and no casualties so far.

As the last member of Company H.Q. had made the far side, a Stuka appeared from behind some trees on the southern side of the bridge, at about fifty feet. Some Brens opened up on it from our side, and several Brownings mounted on our vehicles, on the other; but the Stuka, unruffled and kestrel-like, seemed to hover over the bridge quite patiently, apparently impervious to the hail of lead being directed at it. Then the pilot, having presumably seen all he wished to, made off as suddenly as he had come.

We established our headquarters in a large house which faced the river, and lay back some thirty yards from it on the top of the ridge. It was "covered" at the rear by some outhouses, which 10 Platoon occupied, and farther afield by the odd cottage in which 11 and 12 Platoons based themselves. "H" Company secured our right flank, but the only protection on our left was a section of 9 Platoon, dismounted, of course. They had no hope whatever of holding an attack should one come in from that direction, and again we had to trust to luck. Some 77 mm. guns on the Hussars' Comets on the home side were trained on to our left flank, and it was registered with D.Fs., as was our entire perimeter, but not unnaturally it persisted as a bad headache. A weak flank meant a weak position, but we had insufficient men for complete all-round protection.

We had guessed that the Stuka was carrying out a reconnaissance and we thus expected a more forceful visit some time later. It was not long in coming. About an hour after our last troops had arrived, perhaps a little less, when it was approaching evening, another aircraft came over, very low, and dropped some anti-personnel bombs on our positions, causing casualties in 10 Platoon. They were brought into Company H.Q. house and laid, on their stretchers, in the main entrance hall, where the stetcher-bearers, with many other helpers, attended to their needs as best they could. We all knew evacuation was likely to be delayed, as the Weser separated us from the Regimental Aid Post and further medical help; and the transporting of casualties in assault boats across a river under continual shell-fire, and possible bombing, was bound to take time. Later we heard that Sergt. Wickham had died of his wounds; a very great loss to the Company in both the military and the personal sense.

The Command Post was established in a cellar, one of a series of subterranean rooms in the centre of the house. It was very small, the floor space being about twelve by twelve feet, and with a height of about seven feet. All around the walls were shelves and chests, the former arrayed with vast quantities of preserves, both fruit and vegetable, bottles of Chianti and hams. There was a little table in the centre, and a few chairs, which left a narrow margin of about eighteen inches width for movement around the room. Wireless communication was at the time being maintained by our portable 38 sets, and the aerial rod described a broad arc across the ceiling and half-way down the far wall. The platoon signallers also laid their own lines to their respective positions from a central phone in the Command Post. The battalion signallers laid a line across the river from Battalion H.Q. to the two Company H.Q. and although the line over the water was immediately severed by shell-fire, the lateral link between "G" and "H" proved its worth as the hours went by. The Signal Officer later ferried over a 19 set to us with some batteries, and by nightfull communications were in good order.

The Company, with darkness fallen, was "Normandy-alert." The night was happily quiet, but at nine o'clock the following morning, 11 Platoon rang through to report infantry advancing in waves on to the Company's positions. "Hundreds of 'em," said Clark— "Hundreds of 'em." Over the air, artillery support was immediately enlisted, and the gunners, having previously registered on selected "D.Fs." were able to bring down an almighty "Stonk" slap in the midst of the enemy. The force was, for all purposes, written off, but the Germans, refusing to acknowledge defeat, put in a further attack within a very short time, which turned out to be even more suicidal than the first, thanks very largely to the 25-pdrs. again. What remnants of the Hun that showed themselves afterwards were speedily picked off by 11 Platoon. Kenneth Chabot had been watching the whole show from a top storey window. He came down in great jubilation, rubbing his hands and muttering, "First class—First-class. That'll teach the bloody Boche ! "

By midday the Sappers were making good headway with the bridge despite constant shelling. It was growing hourly, and every span put into position meant to us one link nearer to tank support which we so earnestly desired. But the enemy realized this too, evinced by his never ceasing salvoes of 88 mms. which proved costly to the Sappers. When in the mid-afternoon hopes of achieving our link before dusk were running high, for the bridge was over half-way across, a Stuka appeared and dropped an anti-personnel bomb right amongst the toiling bridge-builders. Eighteen of them were killed outright. Further bombing followed and destroyed their bridge too, which now resembled the original one—just so much twisted metal. There was no sign of the R.A.F. nor had we any heavy Ack-Ack protection. Our own Brens and Brownings chattered constantly against the marauders, but they were quite futile, the tracers visibly bouncing off the armoured bellies of the Boche planes as they swooped low over the rooftops. That bridge had symbolized all our hopes. As one sank, so did the other.

Over in the bridgehead, we were inclined to think that the drivers, who had stayed with their vehicles, and the few other members of the Company who were still on the "right " side, were having a fairly easy time. It was not till we met up with them again later that we began to realize that it had not been all beer and skittles with them. Not a few of the bombs meant for the bridge (or us) had whistled down on their side of the river, and many 88 and 105 overshoots landed amongst them, quite apart from aimed shots at the church tower, which the Boche presumably thought we were using as an Observation Post. One of these overshoots made a direct hit on one of our half-tracks.

Towards evening, in the now untroubled sky, some R.A.F. Tempests put in an appearance, making quite a brave display over the bodies of eighteen dead Sappers and their wrecked bridge.

That night we heard the heartening news that some Commandos were coming across to reinforce us, widen the bridgehead, and then push on to the village of Leese, which lay about 2,000 yards in front of us, and in which the S.S. Troops who were opposing us had based themselves. We were still more encouraged when we heard a whole Commando brigade was coming over. They started arriving from 0200 hrs. onwards and throughout the night until 0600 hrs. they poured into our bridgehead, interrupted only by a counter-attack which developed on "H" Company's position during the small hours. We had, like everybody else, heard a lot about Commandos, but we had never fought with them before; and with all due respect we were amazed, after daylight had broken, to see them walking about, seemingly quite oblivious of the enemy so close at hand, making no effort whatever to conceal their movements. In consequence, a considerable enemy artillery barrage came down on our positions, wounding many of them, some seriously. To us, trained for years in fieldcraft, and concealment of movement, their lack of the same left us speechless. It was, in fairness to them, explained to us afterwards, that Commandos were trained to work by night, when with blackened faces, and soft tread they could well remain undetected. By 0715 hrs. the Commandos had taken over all our positions and the Company was beginning to withdraw across the river. Here "F" Company, most of whom had remained on the home side throughout the action, gave us invaluable help in ferrying back men and equipment. While this was going on, the Boche kept up a rather half-hearted airburst barrage with 88s and 105s. By 0815 hrs. the Company was completely back across the river, having happily suffered no casualties during the withdrawal. It was with a feeling of considerable relief that we touched down on a comparatively friendly bank again, to climb aboard our own vehicles once more, and leave Stoltzenau, with all its grim memories, behind us.

We made our way back to a small village about three miles behind the river, where we joined up with our friends of the 23rd Hussars again, had a good wash and a shave and the first decent meal for two days. Then, just before midday, we moved off to Niendorf, again leaving the 23rd Hussars, another mile or so back, where we rested and reorganized our vehicles—which were in a rather bad state after the action of the previous forty-eight hours. All the halftracks with Brownings mounted upon them had their floors ankle-deep in spent cartridge cases—a silent testimony to the defence put up by the drivers against the air attacks.

We stayed the night at Niendorf, making the best use of our time in clearing up generally and resting; then at 1100 hrs. the following morning—Sunday, the 8th—we moved to join up with "A" Squadron again, who had shifted meantime to the area of Petershagen, some way to the south of Stoltzenau, still close to the Weser. At Petershagen itself, the 6th Airborne, who were on our right flank, had succeeded in throwing a bridge across the river, and here, following the 3rd Royal Tank Regiment, we crossed. With the 3rd Tanks in front of us, we were able to push on without opposition, although the going was a little slow. By nightfall we had reached a village just north-east of Husum, already vacated by the 3rd Tanks, who had pushed farther on. Like all German villages that the Regiment "liberated," it was ablaze from one end to the other, only a few houses being spared. As we approached, we could see the flames leaping in the darkness and smouldering pieces of thatch drifting aimlessly through the air like slow-motion tracer. Our friends had not had time to clear the village properly before their departure, as we soon found out for ourselves. Prisoners were brought out from all sorts of odd places, like under beds and woodpiles and, more conventionally, from the cellars. Most of them seemed scared to death. A notable part in Company H.Q. clearing operations was played by inoffensive Guy, who with a most offensive looking Sten gun swaying at his hip created rather an amusing picture amongst an otherwise serious scene. Three separate searches over the same ground were necessary to account for all our prisoners, so well were they concealed.

The night was uneventful, and at 0640 hrs. the following morning we, "A" Squadron and "G" Company, set off in the lead on the road to Wenden. It was still early when we reached the village, and as we emerged from the far side into some open country, two enemy half-tracks towing 88s were spotted pulling out of the woods. It was apparent that they had not the slightest idea of our presence, and they were easy targets for the 23rd's 77 mm. guns. In three shots, both of them were "brewed up." Another mile or two down the road brought us to the village of Steimbke. It looked peaceful enough, sheltering in a quiet valley under a warm sun in the morning sky. The small cottages, with their thatched roofs, and a small pretty church, presented a picture of complete tranquillity. Incongruously, stiff resistance was encountered here, in the form of a Company of the 12th S.S., armed with bazookas and small arms. 12 Platoon and Sergt. Baldwin's section of carriers, with a troop of tanks in support, went in to clear it.

Soon, however, it was evident that resistance was much too stiff for them and as they moved down the village their rear became seriously menaced. Orders were given for them to withdraw and plans were made to put in a two-company attack on the village, preceded by shelling from our 25-pdrs. and a hail of bombs from our mortar detachment.

Again we advanced into the village and this time it was successful, but not without cost. The S.S. fought fanatically and every house had to be cleared individually. Our stretcher-bearers were fired on which spurred us on even more. No quarter was given or asked and very few S.S. prisoners lived to tell the tale of the battle for Steimbke.

Eric Yetman, who as usual was quite regardless of his personal safety, was wounded and later died. He had been a great inspiration and example to us and his loss was deeply felt by all. Under his leadership, 12 Platoon had accomplished many brave deeds which will never fade in our memory.

Just before darkness fell we collected ourselves together and moved on a few miles to the village of Rodewald. Here we remained for three days, waiting for a bridge to be built across the River Aller.

It was a much-needed pause, as we were all very tired indeed and there was much work to be done in reorganizing, both as regards personnel and equipment.

During this time the 11th Armoured Division began negotiations with Colonel Schmitt, commandant of the now notorious Belsen concentration camp. Stories filtered through to us of the conditions there, but none of us at this time really had the slightest idea of the real significance of this living hell on earth.

On Friday, the 13th of April, we were on the move again, crossing the River Leine at Helsdorf and concentrating a short way farther on at Schwarnstedt. Here we spent the rest of the day and except for the appearance of the odd Stuka from time to time nothing of interest occurred.

The next day we crossed the Aller at Essel and again went into a concentration area to the east of the river.

We had now begun releasing many thousands of Allied prisoners of war, and it was a great sight to see them come streaming into our lines, their faces aglow with excitement at once again being amongst friends. All was done to make them comfortable and help them on their way and we showered on them all the cigarettes and food we could muster. They brought with them tales of utter confusion and chaos amongst the Germans ahead of us. The end was surely well and truly in sight.

Leaving the ploughed fields in which we had laagered at Esse, we moved off after breakfast the next day and advanced through Winsen and Walle, and shortly came to another small village. The yellow German road signs, edged in black, announced "Belsen." It was just another name to us then. The sight of a concentration camp on our left as we drove through caused us no surprise, for through the talks with Colonel Schmitt, we had been warned of its presence. The whole place was surrounded by pretty young conifers, and beyond them a barbed wire fence about twelve feet high. By the entrances which occurred at intervals there stood groups of Hungarian guards—we recognized them by the colour of their uniforms—and small knots of men, pyjama-clad. They were the inmates; those that could still stand. We had been ordered not to fire at enemy personnel in the camps unless we were provoked, as it was common knowledge that the place was alive with typhus, and unnecessary fighting inside the camp would only tend to spread the disease. In consequence, the job of entering and clearing up was left to other units of the Division who were following on behind.

As we left Belsen and pushed on, we little guessed what sights lay concealed behind those trim rows of conifers.

On reaching Bergen we took the lead, and a short way farther on we halted for the night, surrounded by blazing houses for as far as the eye could see. A great number of prisoners were collected, and whilst escorting back a party of these one of our carrier sections was attacked by enemy armed with bazookas. 11 Platoon had to be sent to their aid and the whole party returned to us just before midnight, complete with still more prisoners.

The 16th of April saw us in front of another water obstacle—the River Orge. The 159th Infantry Brigade made a successful crossing at Muden, and after we had run into a certain amount of opposition on our front it was decided to switch us on to the 159th Brigade centre line and across their bridge.

We followed the 3rd Tanks group and a short "swan" developed. By nightfall we had reached the village of Wriedel. Here we settled down for the night. Things were going very well again and our progress during the day had been unexpectedly good. However, it was not long before we were brought to our senses again.

The 15th Scottish Division were approaching Uelsen from the south, and in order to assist their attack on the town, which was thought to be heavily defended, the 11th Armoured Division was to establish itself to the north, thus cutting the Germans' escape route to Luneburg.

We passed through the 3rd Tanks group and pushed on without much difficulty to Seedorf. On leaving the village, however, and on approaching the main Uelsen—Luneburg road, the leading two tanks and the leading carrier were hit and began blazing furiously. The fire was coming from a wood on the main cross-roads, and accompanying the armour-piercing shells was a steady volume of fire from 20 mms. and small arms.

The situation looked unhealthy, as there was no other way of approaching the cross-roads except across a wide expanse of absolutely open country. However, luck was with us, in the shape of a Squadron of Typhoons who were on call. A very short space of time elapsed before they appeared overhead. A few anxious moments followed, as the pink smoke used for indicating their target had been put down erroneously on one of our own positions, but the impending catastrophe was averted. After circling the objective two or three times, down they came, diving to tree-top height and loosing their deadly rockets with incredible accuracy into the midst of the enemy position. We had never before seen these aircraft operate so close ahead of us, and our grandstand, a few hundred yards away, was rocked by the explosions.

To make absolutely sure that the position had been neutralized, we next called on our artillery to bring down a heavy concentration on the wood. and as the last shells of the barrage were bursting we made our way forward again.

This time not a sound came from the wood, and on arriving there we found ample evidence of the destruction wrought by the Typhoons and the guns. Many dead Germans and several wrecked guns were the only testimony of what we had been up against and no live or even wounded German remained to tell the tale.

Turning south, we established ourselves on another cross-roads north of Uelsen, and here we remained for the day in comparative peace and quiet, getting a very good view of the attack on the village of Barum, which was strongly defended. For a long time 11 and 12 Platoons stood by, as it was thought they might be needed to reinforce the assault.

Nothing appeared to be bolting from Uelsen in our direction, and after remaining for the night on our position we were ordered, next morning, to turn north again up the main road to Bienenbuttel, which we reached without any trouble. Then, instead of continuing on to Luneburg, which was only some six miles away, we branched off to the east, making our way through some very close and wooded country, eventually arriving astride the highway running east from the town. Along this road, to our delight, we saw approaching a column of German horse-drawn transport, and it was only a matter of minutes before this ragged procession ceased to exist as such. A certain number of prisoners were taken, and after a short pause we moved on north again, reaching the village of Reinstorf, which we entered after overcoming very slight opposition.

Here we made a firm base and pushed out a carrier and tank patrols who were to try and reach the Elbe, which was now a mere six or seven miles away. On arriving before the village of Neetze, however, they met opposition and, after engaging it for some time, failing light caused the project to be abandoned and they withdrew to us at Reinstorf for the night.

Back with them came a story which later became greatly publicized by the Press and the B.B.C. At Neetze they had liberated Belli's Circus, and I don't think I can do better at this point than quote an eye-witness account of this incident as later broadcast by two of our Riflemen who took part in it.

"We reached Neetze without much difficulty and took up a position on the cross-roads. Everything was peaceful until suddenly from our rear a gun opened up and shells began whizzing by uncomfortably near to us. Eventually a German self-propelled gun was spotted and this was successfully 'brewed up' by the tanks.

"After this incident it was decided to send a section of carriers to make a reconnaissance of the area of the self-propelled gun. The first thing which met their eyes was a collection of vehicles hidden deep in the wood, which they assumed to be German transport. Anyway, deciding not to take any chances, they fired a belt of Browning at these objects. The reply to this were noises which made them think they had suddenly been transported to the jungle, and on closer investigation the supposed German transport proved to be caravans of artistes and animals belonging to Belli's Circus. Unfortunately, there was no time to really get to know the circus folk as darkness was coming on and we had to withdraw to the next village for the night.

"The next day, however, early in the morning, we returned to Neetze, and on hearing the approach of our vehicles, a great reception was prepared for us. The fat lady, the lion tamer, the midgets and countless others turned out to greet us in no uncertain manner. "For the remainder of the day they celebrated their liberation and by the late afternoon were in tremendous from and staggered out to wave goodbye to us. Little did we know then that several months later they would actually give a show for us in our area of occupation."

Our support company joined us for the night in Reinstorf and the hours of darkness passed without incident. Early in the morning, however, a German car drove into the village and was duly shot up by 11 Platoon, although this claim was, and always will be hotly contested by our anti-tank gunners, who blazed away at the wretched car with one of their guns.

Shortly afterwards we all moved on to Neetze, which we entered without opposition, and we again pushed out tank and carrier patrols to cut off any Germans trying to escape from the west. This was a highly profitable move and the rest of the day was spent by these patrols in amassing prisoners, who were mostly only too willing to give themselves up. In addition, just before lunch two American airmen, who had escaped from the Germans, came in and told us that there was a complete company a few miles away, ensconced in farms and merely waiting for someone to come and take them prisoner. James and I, thinking that this might be a very worthwhile mission, accompanied 11 Platoon on an expedition to find this company. Sure enough, this orderly collection of Germans was in the appointed place, complete with all their equipment and stores. After a brief examination of the stores, which interested us more than the men, we returned triumphantly to Company H.Q. with our prize.

After assuming that we would remain where we were for the night, orders came through that we were going to be relieved and that we were to move with the rest of the group to a position west of Luneburg and there act as left flank protection to 8 Corps.

Shortly afterwards the Reconnaissance Regiment of the 15th Scottish Division arrived on the scene and we started on our journey westwards, carrying some two hundred and fifty prisoners on our vehicles.

A brief halt was made outside Luneburg while we dumped off our prisoners, and after passing through the town we eventually arrived at Westergellersen. Our role here did not seem, on closer examination, to be very exacting, and we accordingly made ourselves as comfortable as possible, knowing that we were likely to stay in the village for some days at least.

The advance of the Second Army had been so rapid that obviously the supply situation must have become critical again, but this time the end appeared so near that it seemed likely that risks would be taken. Our assumptions were not far wrong.

CHAPTER XIV

ONE MORE RIVER TO CROSS

THE Elbe had by now been reached by the Allies on a broad front and rumours were current that the Americans had linked up with the Russians. Despite the apparent hopelessness of their position, however, air reconnaissance showed that the Germans on the opposite bank of the river facing us appeared to be preparing to resist hotly any attempt to cross.

Speed was the order of the day, and accordingly a great part of our load-carrying transport was requisitioned to assist the hard-pressed supply services in their superhuman efforts to enable us to cross the Elbe in the shortest possible time. These lorries drove right back to Goch to pick up ammunition and supplies, and it was not long before the now familiar dumps of ammunition were appearing on the verges of the roads leading to the river, while load after load of bridging material streamed up to the places chosen for the assault.

While all this was going on we spent a very pleasant and peaceful week at Westergellersen, and no warlike activities were undertaken except in the case of the carriers, who helped to clear a sector of the Forest of Munster without incident.

Otherwise maintenance and cleaning up were our main activities, as well as a certain amount of football. Life went on quietly and we expected to stay in this village until our time came to cross the Elbe, so it came as somewhat of a surprise to us when we were suddenly ordered to move to Winsen to take over from the Herefords.

This town was some miles from the river bank, and except for very occasional shelling was a peaceful and pleasant enough spot. Everyone was billeted very comfortably and we began to realize why the Herefords were not very enthusiastic about being relieved from their front-line position. We had, however, to have one forward post at Hoopte, which was on the river bank, and German patrols had been fairly active in that area.

When our turn came to supply the "Hoopte Force," it was made up of 12 Platoon and a section of carriers, with Kenneth Chabot in command. The latter had previously been rather shaken by a platoon commander of the Herefords showing him the scars on one of his legs, caused by a bazooka. However, nothing happened during the tour of duty of our force and they returned to us safe and sound the following night.

On the 30th of April we were relieved in the early morning by a battalion of the Welch Regiment from 53rd Division and we made our way back to Westergellersen to rejoin the 23rd Hussars. The crossing of the Elbe had already been made by the 15th Scottish Division, and the 11th Armoured Division was expected to move up and go through them at any minute.

However, it was not until half-past four in the afternoon that we set forth on our drive through Luneburg to the village of Artienburg, where we were to cross the Elbe. The traffic jams on the road were quite appalling and progress was painfully slow.

The light was fading well before we reached the bridge as we moved a few yards at a time, nose to tail in the unending column of vehicles. We could see ahead in the sky the ceaseless patrolling of R.A.F. fighters over the bridge, but we knew that once darkness came on they would have to return to their bases. So we prayed that we would cross the bridge before the last patrol left for home. But it was not to be and it was late in the night before we had moved forward the remaining few miles to the river bank.

It was a very dark night, but we were aided by artificial moonlight and we were most fortunate in the complete absence of enemy interference from the air. Not long after we had crossed, however, the Luftwaffe arrived, but had no luck in destroying the bridge.

The advance continued northwards all through the night and it was not long before we had reached the farthest forward positions of the 15th Scottish.

The idea of going through these positions, not knowing what we were likely to meet or anything about the countryside through which we were passing, was not a pleasant one, but orders were orders and on we went, experiencing a certain amount of difficulty in reading our maps.

About an hour before light came, as we were moving forward, closed up, along a country road, the noise of violent explosions rent the night air, accompanied by vivid flashes. The leading two tanks were "brewing" as also was one of our carriers. In addition, another carrier had been hit but had not caught fire. The column was also engaged by small-arms fire and altogether the situation appeared very tricky. We could not see where the enemy were and could only guess that the heavy stuff had come from a tank or self-propelled gun farther down the road. Obviously nothing could be done till daylight came, and we accordingly settled ourselves down in all-round defence, anxiously awaiting the arrival of the dawn. On looking at our maps we found we were just short of the village of Sahms.

As soon as we were able to see what we were doing, we rapidly dispersed our vehicles in the neighbouring fields, as our jammed-up column would have presented a heaven-sent target to a well-sited armoured fighting vehicle or gun.

As soon as daylight arrived, I sent Neil Hughes-Onslow and a party from 11 Platoon out on patrol to try and get some information as to what was in the village of Sahms. From our maps we could see a stream ran through the far end of the village, and we were anxious to know whether the bridge across this was still intact. In the meantime we made provisional plans for clearing Sahms with the aid of the tanks, as it seemed obvious that this would have to be done in the end. We also had time to prepare a hasty breakfast, which was most welcome after the sleepless night we had just spent. At this stage our hopes of an early victory faded well into the background.

Over an hour passed and we began to wonder what had happened to Neil's patrol. He had taken out a wireless with him, but after a short while communication failed and so we had not the slightest idea as to his whereabouts.

Suddenly a line of figures hove into sight and we saw with amazement and at first with apprehension that they were mostly clad in field grey. Our fears were soon set at rest, however, when Neil himself appeared wandering along with an air of nonchalance as if he was returning from a stroll in the country.

He told me an incredible story. He had been moving down the side of a lane with his patrol, clinging to the hedgerows for cover, when there appeared in the distance a marching column. The patrol lay low in a ditch at the side of the road, expecting each moment to be their last, and the column, which turned out to be a German battalion, although it was only approximately sixty in strength, drew level with them. By this time Neil had noticed that there were some ten stragglers, so, letting the main body pass by, he and his men emerged from the ditch, and held up these extremely surprised Germans who had been lagging behind. One of these turned out to be the Battalion Commander himself and so, thinking they had accomplished enough for the moment, they had returned with their collection of prisoners.

The Battalion Commander who was only too willing to talk, gave us the information that two battalions, both about sixty strong, were moving into Sahms. So it seemed quite clear that the sooner we got cracking into the village before the enemy had had time to organize any defence the better it would be for us.

Our prearranged plans were accordingly quickly checked over and 10 and 12 Platoons, supported by a troop of tanks, prepared themselves for battle. After a very heavy barrage from our artillery, we moved forward to the assault. On the way into the village a car dashed out and tried to escape down a side road, but its effort was in vain. It was completely shattered by a shell fired from one of the tanks. Soon after we had entered the village, Germans came running out of houses to give themselves up and it was by now quite clear that they had not even made a start on any defensive preparations. One isolated bit of resistance was soon cleared up and by the time we had reached the far end of the village we found ourselves with some sixty prisoners on our hands. Our shelling had also taken its toll and several dead Germans lay about as a silent testimony to its effectiveness.

The bridge over the stream was very badly damaged, but we

reckoned that by putting in some hard work on it we could make it serviceable enough to get all our vehicles across. The labour for this task was conveniently at hand in the shape of the prisoners, and organizing them into parties we set them to work. No threats or encouragement were needed and they set to work with tremendous energy and enthusiasm, just as if they were building a vital bridge for themselves.

Unfortunately it was not long before a battery of 88 mm. guns got wind of our activities and an extremely unpleasant period of spasmodic shelling followed, which was accurate enough to suggest that we were being observed. Luckily no shells actually landed on the bridge, although some were very near misses, and none of our work was undone.

The situation was very strange as during the shelling we lay alongside our prisoners, all flat on our faces on the bed of the stream and all as frightened as each other. In between the shelling, however, work went on with unabated vigour and we were soon able to report back that we considered that the stream could now be crossed by tanks. An officer of the Royal Engineers who was sent to check our statement, made some extremely disparaging and unkind remarks about our work and said we should never get anything across, but we realized this to be professional jealousy and we managed to convince our superiors of this.

A short time later along came the column and, although the issue at times seemed in doubt, everyone crossed safely, and we saw no more of the doubting Sapper.

The prisoners who all looked extremely weary, had now served their purpose and we passed them back to a stage nearer the luxuries of a prisoner-of-war cage.

By that time the groups had passed through us, and we found ourselves in reserve. Quite a long time elapsed before we were ordered to move on and we used it to good advantage to clean ourselves up and get some much-needed rest. The day so far had been unpleasant—I would go so far as to say one of the most unpleasant since crossing the Rhine—and little did we realize then that we had to all intents and purposes seen our last action.

When the signal to advance came we moved forward, taking care to keep to the centre of the roads after seeing for ourselves several vehicles badly shattered by mines. The Germans at that stage had buried many bombs intended for aerial warfare, and the occupants of an average vehicle exploding one of these had very little chance of escaping serious injury.

As the day drew to a close we found ourselves on a very poor track leading through some woods to the village of Borstorf. The group in front of us had become bogged, and as there was no hope of getting past them we had to close up our column and settle down for the night beside our vehicles.

Nothing happened to disturb us and those of us who were not on guard slept very soundly after the previous day's exertions. As soon as it was light enough, however, we moved on to some fields just beyond Borstorf, where we settled down to await the arrival of our much-needed supply column. As usual, this turned up as scheduled and, besides the necessary warlike materials, with it came some most welcome and overdue mail.

We were just conjecturing as to what our next move would be when through came the astounding orders that we were to follow the Fife and Forfar group in a bid to seize the port of Lubeck. Stories came through that citizens of Lubeck had cycled out to meet the leading troops and had volunteered to ride on the tanks into the heart of the city. This sounded too good to be true and we felt that there must be a snag somewhere. Our doubts were soon dispelled, however, as when we were just about to set out on what we considered would be a most hazardous venture the sensational news came over the air that the Fifes were already in Lubeck and had met no opposition whatever.

Revised orders quickly came through that we were to proceed with all possible speed to the north of the city to cut all escape routes from it. Engines roared and in an incredibly short space of time our column was hurtling towards its objective, some twenty miles distant. The climax came when we reached the Hamburg-Lubeck autobahn and we streamed down it two vehicles abreast, everyone being in tremendous form. Not a shot was fired and we reached our prearranged positions, where we quickly established ourselves. A small amount of sniping was encountered at one of these, but it was soon quelled and we settled down to the monotonous though lucrative task of collecting literally thousands of dejected German prisoners and hundreds of vehicles of all sizes and sorts. High ranking officers were "two a penny," and none of them seemed to doubt the fact that the war was well and truly over.

As fast as we disposed of enormous columns of prisoners, so we collected fresh ones, and as darkness came on we packed off our last large batch and made an enclosure for the streams we expected to pour in all through the night.

To add to our embarrassment, a party of German A.T.S. girls were brought into my headquarters and promptly passed out. Whether this was a put-up job I will never know, but the fact remains that we had to carry the wretched girls to an upstairs room, where we laid them on the floor alongside the sleeping bodies of the headquarter personnel. To an outsider, who was unaware of the circumstances prevailing, the scene must have looked highly irregular, and he would have been justified in suspecting that fraternisation had started in a very big way. But all was above board, and at the earliest opportunity, the girls were removed to a neighbouring house.

Most of the next day was spent in the same place amassing hundreds more prisoners and immeasurable quantities of booty. One particular item of interest was a brand new "Jagd Panther" with a "super 88 millimetre" gun. A round was in the breach and it was covering the road down which we had moved the previous day. This formidable armoured fighting vehicle could have wrought havoc amongst our column had it really tried, and we could only imagine that either the crews' courage must have failed at the last moment or that the firing mechanism of the gun had been at fault. Whichever alternative was the right one, however, we had had a very fortunate escape.

About teatime we bade farewell to Lubeck after an exciting but very tiring stay and made our way westwards about ten miles to the little village of Strukdorf, where we settled into some quite comfortable quarters and where our operational commitments were not exactly arduous. Rumours of peace were rife, but having suffered so many disappointments in the past, we preferred to curb our spirits until something official came through.

Late in the evening orders were given for a move to Kiel in the morning and the more optimistic of us hoped it might be a repetition of the entry into Lubeck.

The morning of the 4th of May dawned and a signal came through postponing our move for twenty-four hours. This surely signified that something was in the air and gave us something really concrete on which to base our speculations.

No more news, however, came through and we spent a quiet, peaceful day where we were. The weather was warm and sunny enough to lie out in the garden and read, write and sleep and we took full advantage of it.

The last few hours of the 4th of May will remain clear in our memories for ever. We were sitting in our headquarters, with the wireless booming out dance music. Suddenly a little before nine o'clock the music stopped and all was quiet. Then the voice of the announcer rang out—you could have heard a pin drop in the room. "The German Armies facing the 21st Army Group have surrendered to Field-Marshal Montgomery," he announced. We gasped—it was the news we had waited for for over five and a half years. All at once the tension relaxed and everyone went crazy with joy. We had to give vent to our feelings. Parachute flares from mortars, Very lights and tracer bullets were soon making a crazy pattern in the sky, and people were madly rushing about shaking hands with each other and slapping each other on the back.

Fantastic rejoicing went on till the early hours and every drop of liquor accumulated during the past months was soon exhausted. I well remember one of my Sergeants, who deeply resented his nickname of "Tojo," coming up to me, throwing his arms around me and begging me to sing the Japanese National Anthem with him.

As we eventually retired to rest that night, some in prearranged resting-places and some not, I think many of us felt our limbs to make sure that we were still in possession of them all and offered up a prayer of gratitude that we had been spared to live through this great occasion. So many had not.

EPILOGUE

LITTLE remains to be told of our warlike activities. After a week at Strukdorf, during which we prepared to move several times to various places, we heard that our final resting-place was to be Schleswig.

On the 12th May we moved into Schloss Gottorf, an old Danish castle, used by the Germans as a cavalry barracks. The place was in a filthy state and very typical of all German military premises. However, it was not long before we made it habitable, after taking great delight in supervising the Germans in the work of cleaning up their own mess.

A new Army life lay ahead of us. The days of free-and-easy living with no questions asked were over. In their place once more we would return to peace time soldiering and all the attendant formalities. Ceremonial guard mounting drill, blancoing, brass cleaning—these were merely a few of the things we once again were to have to stomach and face with cheerful countenance. No more "brew cans" and the attendant odd collection of pots and pans—a lot of old familiar habits we were going to miss. But weighing everything up, it would be hypocritical to say that we were sorry in any way that our days of action were over. We were profoundly thankful.

Schleswig seemed to be a very pleasant place; it was summer and we felt that we had earned some sort of summer holiday. We took it.

And so eleven months, packed with thrills and boredom, interest and fears, had come to a close. None of us would like to live them through again, and yet on the other hand I don't think there are many of us, who, on looking back, would have missed it for the world. Lasting friendships had been cemented both amongst ourselves and amongst the many people we had met in the liberated countries.

I would like to end my attempt at chronicling our story by defining some of the factors which contributed so much towards our good fortune and success.

Undoubtedly one of the foremost factors was the luck we had in having such fine leaders. General "Pip" Roberts was an inspiration to us all. His youth and vitality were in keeping with the spirit of adventure which existed throughout the entire 11th Armoured Division. I don't think any division can ever have had a more admired, popular and respected commander than General "Pip."

Going further down the scale, the 29th Armoured Brigade was just as fortunate in its commander in Brigadier Roscoe Harvey.

Long in our memories will remain the sight of that familiar red-hatted figure protruding from the turret of his tank.

But above all nothing could have been achieved without the individual effort of every single man. Countless unrecorded and, in many cases, unnoticed deeds of bravery would fill volume after volume. The real factor, however, was the wonderful team-work, which never wavered for one moment and without which all would have been in vain.

A small collection of Londoners had set out on a mission; they had been given the tools and they had finished the job.

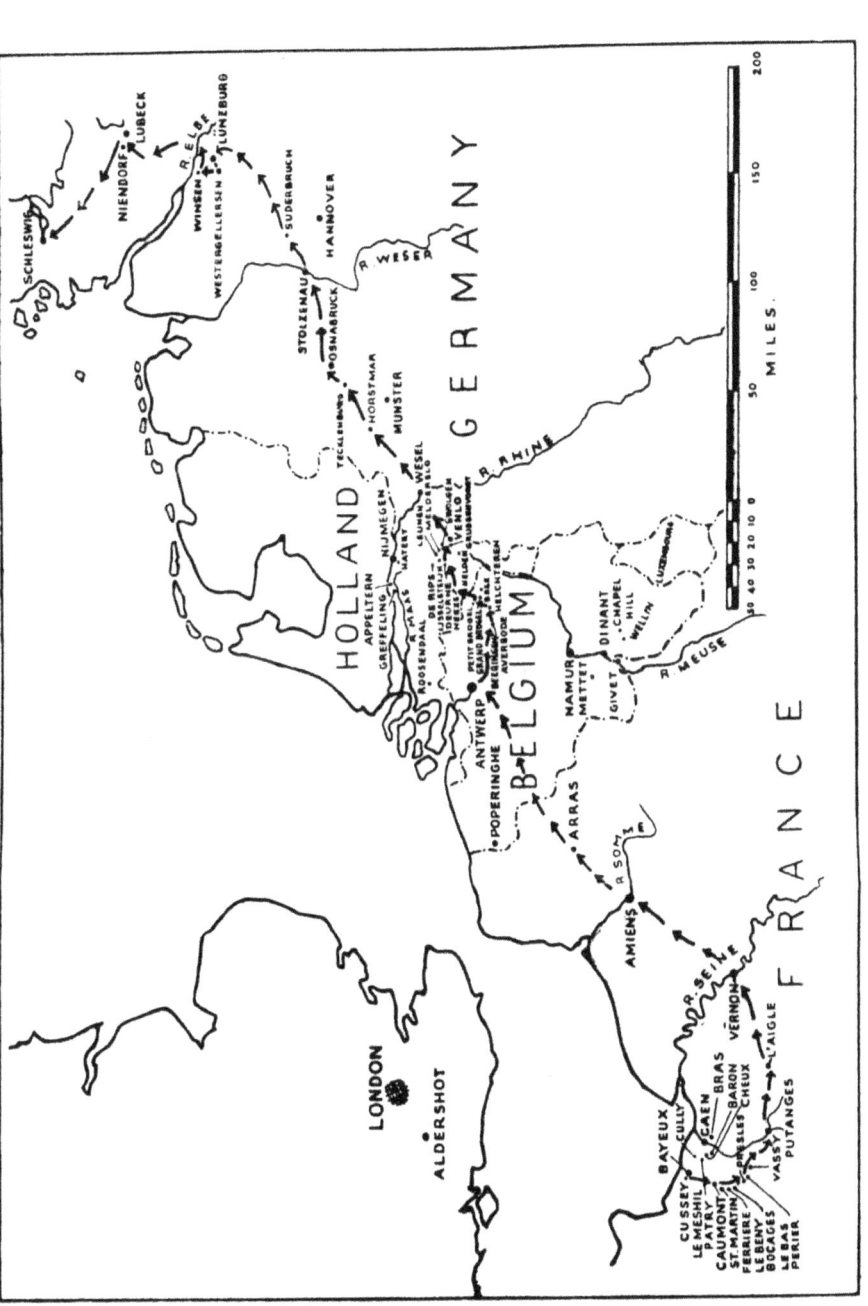

www.ingramcontent.com/pod-product-compliance
Lightning Source LLC
Chambersburg PA
CBHW041927090426
42743CB00021B/3467